NO ARCHIVE WILL RESTORE YOU

Before you start to read this book, take this moment to think about making a donation to punctum books, an independent non-profit press

@ https://punctumbooks.com/support

If you're reading the e-book, you can click on the image below to go directly to our donations site. Any amount, no matter the size, is appreciated and will help us to keep our ship of fools afloat. Contributions from dedicated readers will also help us to keep our commons open and to cultivate new work that can't find a welcoming port elsewhere. Our adventure is not possible without your support.

Vive la Open Access.

Fig. 1. Hieronymus Bosch, *Ship of Fools* (1490–1500)

First published in 2018 by 3Ecologies Books/Immediations, an imprint of punctum books.
https://punctumbooks.com

ISBN-13: 978-1-947447-85-1 (print)
ISBN-13: 978-1-947447-86-8 (ePDF)

LCCN: 2018958567
Library of Congress Cataloging Data is available from the Library of Congress

Book design: Vincent W.J. van Gerven Oei
Cover image: Simryn Gill, *Let go, lets go* (2013). Courtesy of the artist.

HIC SVNT MONSTRA

Julietta Singh

No

Archive

Will

Restore

You

Contents

The starting-point of critical elaboration is the consciousness of what one really is, and is "knowing thyself" as a product of the historical processes to date, which has deposited in you an infinity of traces, without leaving an inventory.... Therefore it is imperative at the outset to compile such an inventory.

— Antonio Gramsci

Acknowledgments

This book could not have done without the friendship, insights, and interventions of: Lisa Smirl, Julie Penner, Cecily Marcus, Sapana Doshi, Ann Pellegrini, Katie Gentile, Jack Halberstam, Macarena Gómez-Barris, Aaron Carico, Allyson Rainer, Susan Wolver, Justin Linds, Jesse Goldstein, Arran Gaunt, Molly Fair, Jagat N. Singh, Christine Common, Giovanni Geremia, and Renate Singh.

Eileen Joy and Vincent W.J. van Gerven Oei embraced this oddball text and offered it a home in the radical land of punctum books. For this remarkable fact, and for being the most badass publishing duo, I thank them so truly.

Then one extraordinary day Erin Manning floated into my world, followed by Brian Massumi, who together understood everything. For simply being, and for folding the book into their 3Ecologies series at punctum, my love and thanks are endless.

Several amazing women shared their sensitivity and enthusiasm for this book at various stages: Thank you especially to Maggie Nelson, Nuar Alsadir, and Orla Mc Hardy. An enormous thanks to Barbara Browning for her support, and for offering a reader response to this book in the form of a weird and wonderful meditation that let me see the book in strange new ways. Thank you to Simryn Gill for permission to use her gorgeous work as cover art for this book.

I am forever and infinitely thankful to Nathan Snaza, who quite simply holds the world together: for fabricating time and space, for reading me endlessly, for all these years of unbelievable friendship. And to Isadora Singh – herself a stunning little archive – always gathering up and transforming every little thing, including me.

No Archive became manifest through magical encounters with my misfit wonder, Silas Howard. For your infinite inspiration and your extraordinary sensitivity in the world, this book is for you.

A Thief, a Desire

IT WAS 2004 AND unapologetically frigid in Minneapolis. The radio had pronounced it the coldest day of the year, though I had learned by then to trust nothing that came from news channels. The heat in my studio apartment was out again, and I was bundled indoors in woolly socks, long johns, and a bulky coat watching my breath billowing out of my body in smoky plumes. My building had been robbed twice within the past week, though my apartment had been magically spared. This is not quite true, because the intruder had in fact come to my door and taken from my doormat my sole pair of sneakers. He had been at the threshold, not quite inside my home but at its border. And he had taken something from that borderland, something that held value for us both. In this sense, it seemed to me that we were undeniably linked. Despite the fact that he had not entered my space, I could feel him palpably inside – not only in the fearful sense of anticipating his return, but in the sense that some trace of him had been left behind, had made its way across the threshold and into that tiny frozen space that had become my makeshift American home.

Anticipating that the thief would strike again, I searched the apartment trying to evaluate what else of mine might be seen as valuable to him. Attempting to abate my fear,

I decided the ethical move was not to defend against him but to find a way to welcome him, to make his forced entry feel less violating. I put a post-it note in the fridge affixed to a can of Red Bull that read Please Feel Free. The note was a strange welcome to my unwanted intruder; an offering of something that it would not hurt me to lose. In fact, the Red Bull was the remnant of some other visitor, someone I had already forgotten who had left behind an item I would never consume. I knew there was an ethical flaw at work in my act of strange hospitality, of offering something to my intruder that I myself did not want. I was deep in self-critique even before the sticky had stuck; I was young and cold and could feel my body aging.

As a brown Canadian kid, I had imagined America as a two-headed monster. One head was a gleaming blond-haired boy with a mouthful of exotic American candies, a big perverse smile chewing unrelentingly. The other head was cloaked in the clownish headgear of the Ku Klux Klan.

I found both heads silly and terrifying; both in different ways seemed to want to devour me.

I came to the United States to study, urged by keen Canadian professors that a PhD in hand from an American university would make me "golden" upon return. I came with hesitancy, never once considering that I might not return, that moving south would over time transform me into an expatriate. When that frigid day in Minneapolis had come to pass, I had been living in America for months and no longer envisioned the nation as a monster. In fact, I had grown to love monsters, recognizing their social function as the abject edges of society. The creation of the monster, I had discerned, is a way of crafting an outside so that a collective can imagine itself as bounded, cohesive, and impenetrable. The monster is a being who will not or cannot fit normally, whose existence makes others uncomfortable and who therefore must be shunned and exiled. No, America was not a monster, though it was highly skilled at creating monstrous figures and exerting force against them. My intruder-guest felt like a monster – like something lurking at the edges of what I had come to believe was properly mine. Something that threatened to come inside, and in so doing to force me to reckon with my relation to it.

Waiting to be robbed is like waiting for an imminent accident in which both you and your assailant are together in disaster. Your assailant in that single moment wields more control, and in response you become in a sense other to yourself. You cannot uphold the usual fantasy of being a self-governing body; you are palpably exposed. I responded to this crisis of being by doing what I always do in moments of critical uncertainty. I did what I had come to America to do: I studied.

I constructed a makeshift nest on my ratty old orange sofa, aesthetically a cross between a bus seat and a church pew. The cushioning inside was endlessly disintegrating, leaving piles of dust beneath it that spread across the floor like a listless diaspora. But I loved the look of that sofa and in any case had no funds to replace it. I was burrowing myself between blankets, flipping through the pages of a foundational work of postcolonial studies, Edward Said's *Orientalism*, when I came upon a passage written by the Italian neo-Marxist political theorist, Antonio Gramsci:

> The starting-point of critical elaboration is the consciousness of what one really is, and is "knowing thyself" as a product of the historical processes to date, which has deposited in you an infinity of trac-

es, without leaving an inventory... Therefore it is imperative at the outset to compile such an inventory.[1]

An infinite history of traces without an inventory! An endless collection of oneself that is impossible to gather... I had no concrete idea of what it meant, or what currency it had in my own life, but I knew how it *felt*. It felt as though the broken thing I was might be restored, and it felt like an embodied idea I would never stop desiring for myself and for the world.

The heat kicked back on in the middle of the night. I could hear the strange clanking of the radiators fumbling back to life. But by then, it was not the double threat of freezing and burglary that left me sleepless, but the opaque and desperately seductive idea of my own impossible archive.

1   Antonio Gramsci, *Selections from the Prison Notebooks,* ed. Quintin Hoare and Geoffrey Nowell Smith (New York: International Publications, 1997), 324. Cited in Edward Said, *Orientalism* (New York: Vintage, 1979), 25.

THERE ARE AT LEAST two ways to understand the emergence of a desire: one is through a moment, when something shifts and the way you act and react, the way you turn things over, is fundamentally altered. The other is through accrual, how over time and repetition our histories draw us toward certain practices and ways of feeling and wanting. My desire is the idea of the archive. Or, more accurately, it is the idea of what the archive might have to offer. While I know that my desire for the archive is in reality a long accrual, I imagine it as this single solitary moment.

desires —
accrual

No Archive Will Restore You

We were scrambling toward the archive. We knew it was crucial, but I suspect that few of us knew what it meant, or where it was, or what to do with it.

We were graduate students in a small cultural theory program, plummeting deeper and deeper into debt, which is in a sense its own hellish kind of archive. We were hoping to be one of the rare exceptions that would be plucked into that almost mythical land of tenure-track work. The job market had undeniably tanked, and a PhD had radically changed over time from being a gateway into stable academic employment to being a credential with almost no real currency in the world. As the university became more and more corporatized and increasingly driven by exploited labor, it was also churning us out in droves, spitting us into a world of highly competitive and highly unstable employment.

Most of us would become underpaid adjunct laborers without access to healthcare, facing our mid-30s without a clear sense of what it had all been for. We told ourselves there was nothing else we would rather do than to study, to be trained into cultural critique over the course of a decade. And it was mostly true. We were trying to stay in solidarity with each other as we competed for scarce fellowships and dwindling jobs, watching the cohorts ahead of us fail to live out the promise of it all, wondering in more and less public ways why we had started down this anxiety-riddled road in the first place.

Why *did* we stay on, with the odds so stacked against us? I don't blame the archive per se, but it undoubtedly held out a kind of promise for each of us that kept us tethered to academia. The archive was an elusive hope of our individual salvation. If we could find the right archive, the right stash of materials that was sexy enough to sell ourselves, we could be spared the depression, the anxiety attacks, the pre-mid-life crises that would come when, one by one, we realized we were not going to be chosen. When, in the face of that brutal rejection, we had no idea what the fuck to do with ourselves. If only we could stumble upon the right archive, the secrets that no one else had yet discovered, we might still be one of the chosen ones. The archive was an opaque hope, yet it kept slipping away as though it didn't want to be found, plundered, excavated. It became outright seductive in its evasiveness, and it kept making clear that it didn't want our masturbatory desire for it. The archive was pure tease, and we were unabashedly shoving borrowed dollar bills down its skimpy thong.

If you are like me and you didn't roll into graduate school knowing the highfalutin importance of the archive, you learn it the moment you step into the seminar room. There, everyone is required to pretend to have one, and everyone wants to know yours. "What's *your* archive?" you'll be asked repeatedly, and your answer will reveal how seriously you should be taken. You learn quickly that "archive" in this context can mean almost anything. In its most obvious iteration, the archive might be a physical place where a collection of documents is housed.

(It behooves me here to admit that I have almost no experience of the brick and mortar archive, that in fact I have a long history of becoming discomfortingly overwhelmed in spaces that contain masses of information. Since childhood, I have felt like a shrunken mind that knows too little, that cowers like a beaten dog each time I am confronted by vast architectures of knowledge.)

But "archive" has more expansive meanings too, which can signal a body of literature (as in the literature of a group of politically motivated writers in South Asia between the 1930s–1960s), or a series of monuments, or a collection of images... In other words, "archive" in graduate school simply means what you are studying, and calling what you study an "archive" gives it heft, grants it the status of an intellectual pursuit. Your archive is an expected declaration – a pronouncement that makes manifest your worth and belonging in the great halls of higher learning. The archive, it must be noted, is also your enabling fiction: it is the thing you *say* you are doing well before you are actually doing it, and well before you understand what the stakes are of gathering and interpreting it.

"NOTHING IS LESS RELIABLE, nothing is less clear today than the word 'archive,'" writes Jacques Derrida,[1] who begins his meditation on the archive (and its particular relation to psychoanalysis) by turning us to *arkhē,* the linguistic root of the word. *Arkhē,* Derrida explains, articulates both commencement and commandment. In the first iteration, *arkhē* is the place from which everything emerges, the location from which the thoughts and things of the world spring forth. In the second, it is the place of authoritative law, from where authority is exercised and externalized. How, the philosopher asks, can we hold these two meanings together? What is this place – the archive – where the beginning of things and the authority to govern over them both emerge? For Derrida, the archive is troubling; it marks a series of secrets between the public and the private, but also and most intimately, "between oneself and oneself."[2]

Early in his famous book *Archive Fever,* Derrida worries over the novelty and value of his meditation on the archive, pausing to confess from the outset that

> in the end I have nothing new to say. Why detain
> you with these worn-out stories? Why this wasted
> time? Why archive this? Why these investments in
> paper, in ink, in characters? Why mobilize so much
> space and so much work, so much typographical
> composition? Does this merit printing? Aren't these
> stories to be had everywhere?[3]

Derrida's rumination on the archive turns out for him to be an irresolvable problem from which a whole host of

1   Jacques Derrida, *Archive Fever: A Freudian Impression,* trans. Eric Prenowitz (Chicago & London: University of Chicago Press, 1996).
2   Ibid., 90.
3   Ibid., 9.

intellectual projects sprung forth. Did they offer some-thing new? Did they merit printing? Whether or not this proliferation of Derridean archival engagements were themselves useful expenditures I cannot say. To be sure, I have never understood how to constitute usefulness. But most certainly they became part of the archive's archive, marking a moment in intellectual history when none of us understood the archive, and none of us could stop reaching for it.

Is it too bold to say that the time of the archive has passed? The archive as an intellectual desire seems by now to be cliché. *Cliché*. A senior professor in graduate school once told me off-handedly that "cliché" is a French onomatopoeia, originating from the sound produced by a particular kind of printing. The sound of something be-ing repeatedly reproduced. Our professional relationship had briefly turned into a silly affair – something entirely predictable and utterly foolish. As I watched his mouth sound out the definition of cliché, I wondered if he knew that he was commenting on our relational breach.

Years later when I confessed with deep shame to a femi-nist mentor that I had done something so utterly cliché as having an affair with a male professor, she replied: "But of course it's cliché! It's cliché because it is continuously reproduced! You are part of a reproductive machine!" It is a story that is "to be had everywhere," the gendered pow-er dynamics of intellectual mentorship. I was fully aware and critical of these dynamics, and fully reproduced them while imaging myself as unique. Just as our archival chase seems to reproduce a structure of knowledge over and over and over again.

WHEN AN ARCHIVIST FRIEND recently visited my home, she noticed stacks of books on the archive scattered about the living room and asked me pointedly over my investment in it. She had just returned from a radical archivist conference in Oregon, where archivists decried the scholarly preoccupation with the site of their impassioned labor. For them, the critique of the archive's gaps and silences fails to account for their low wages, and for the lack of accessibility to some of the materials they most want to gather. What's more, my friend declares, they are also affronted by the lack of scholarly attention to the archivist's own ideas.

In the face of the archivist's frustration, how do I respond? Writers often balk in those moments when they must explain in quick snippets what they are writing about. We work in words yet struggle to make language capture our engagements. I am someone who writes to understand what I think; I write what I do not yet know how to place into language and thought.

Confronted with the archivist's frustration, I respond awkwardly that my interest in the archive is more creative than intellectual. This is a lie, since I cannot parse the difference between these modes. I say, also, that my passion for the archive is rooted in the suspicion that its time has passed; it feels already like an intellectual remnant.

If the archive is a remnant, it is one that keeps whispering to me, insisting on its place in my everyday life. What I might have said to her instead is this: "I am a disquieted archive that fumbles in words. A thing made up of infinite, intractable traces."

Or, I might simply have said: "The archive is a stimulus between myself and myself."

C HAD JUST RETURNED from a year of research in Argentina when I met her in my first year of graduate school. She had a no-nonsense sensibility and a rare brisk walking pace that perfectly matched my own. She was several years ahead of me in her PhD, writing about Argentine women who, as political prisoners during the last dictatorship, stored subversive literature in their vaginal canals. She called this "the vaginal library." Both metaphor and place, the vaginal library seemed to me an embodied archive in organic ruin. It brought the notion of "preservation" into the cell in a doubled sense: into those cages that imprisoned women, and into the cellular structures of their bodies.

Truth be told, I have never once since then heard the word "archive" without thinking immediately of dissenting vaginas. These two things – archive and vagina – have become sutured in my thought.

I learned from C about these dissenting Argentine women just after the building burglaries, after I had stumbled on Gramsci's summons to compile an inventory of historical traces. It was then that I started to wonder over my own body as an impossible, deteriorating archive – a body that had across my life felt both excessive and insufficient, oftentimes even monstrous. Abandoning the pursuit of a legitimate archive – one external to me and one that might ensure my professional success and upward mobility – I began instead to dwell on the messy, embodied, illegitimate archive that I am.

The Body Archive

Why this desire for a body archive, for an assembly of history's traces deposited in me? (I worry over how to describe it, how to frame it without sounding banal or bafflingly idiosyncratic.) The body archive is an attunement, a hopeful gathering, an act of love against the foreclosures of reason. It is a way of knowing the body-self as a becoming and unbecoming thing, of scrambling time and matter, of turning toward rather than against oneself. And vitally, it is a way of thinking-feeling the body's unbounded relation to other bodies.

I begin then to compile an archive of my body, an activity that from the start feels discomfortingly intimate. Too intimate and too bewildering an undertaking, because like all other bodies mine has become so many things over time, has changed dramatically through forces both natural and social. I am also, it must be noted, a person whose body has been broken and maimed many times over – a fact that I cannot yet entirely account for.

How, then, to undertake this desired body archive? There are, of course, those obvious places that are marked on the body, places where the body has been cut, or burned, or broken. I could begin simply by cataloguing these inflictions through the traces they have left behind. Just as easily, I could also turn to my body's naturally occurring oddities, the ways that it has grown and developed against perceived social norms. Both approaches emphasize the body's surface, and both dwell on its "imperfections" – those aspects that we (especially those of us trained as women) see magnified so acutely that when we look at ourselves we see not body but flaw, not the histories that produced us but a catalogue of deficiency.

While these topographical oddities may indeed become part of my archive, they cannot constitute its core. This is in part because I do not want to gather a body archive strictly in order to convert culturally produced deficiency into historical value; to begin to love, in other words, what I have been trained to perceive as flaw.

There is an archival crisis already looming here, because the body's surface is ultimately not stable ground upon which to build an archive. While the skin is a visual sign of the body's exterior limit, the physicist Karen Barad emphasizes how in fact bodies extend into space well beyond the skin. Molecularly, we spread into the "outside" world, mingling with it in ways that are not apparent to us. Our bodies are porous, as Nancy Tuana reminds us when she calls into question "the boundaries between our flesh and the flesh of the world."[1] These feminist formulations of the body insist on our vital entanglements with the outside world, complicating any easy binary demarcations of "inside" and "outside." For better and for worse, we are made up of an outside world which constitutes, nourishes, and poisons us in turns.

1   Nancy Tuana, "Viscous Porosity," in *Material Feminisms,* eds. Stacy Alaimo and Susan Hekman, 188–213 (Bloomington: Indiana University Press, 2008), 198.

This is not only a material problem for my body archive, but also an affective one. In the end, we are not bounded, contained subjects, but ones filled up with foreign feelings and vibes that linger and circulate in space, that enter us as we move through our lives. We likewise leave traces of ourselves and our own affective states (which are never really just our own) behind us when we go. After all the discipline we have endured to teach us that we are self-governing and self-contained, responsible for how we feel, Teresa Brennan insists that "the taken-for-grantedness of the emotionally contained subject is a residual bastion of Eurocentrism in critical thinking."[2] How we think about ourselves as material and emotional beings turns out to be a style of thought, one that emerges from a specific place (Europe) at a specific time (modernity). Against this historically imposing style of thought, I am fully invested in the conviction that our bodies and minds are less discrete than we have been led to believe. Bodies and minds: I confess, I have already lost the difference between them.

There is something haunting to me about the fact that I lean on contemporary feminist new materialist discourse to account for the fact that the body is not and has never been singular. Something haunting about the fact that the non-singularity of the body, its vital entanglements with other kinds of bodies, was once so obvious across cultures, geographies, and histories that it didn't need to be argued. Something changed, something *was* changed. A monumental worldview swept in and tried – with brute force, with discipline, with pedagogy – to make us each one self. But there is a prolific past that tells a different story of the body as an infinite collection of bodyings. And the grand historical force of producing the singular

2   Teresa Brennan, *The Transmission of Affect* (Ithaca: Cornell University Press, 2004), 2.

31

self has made these pasts difficult to gather, difficult to archive.

Pondering the idea of the body archive, I cannot resist thinking toward those palpable bodily openings: the orifices. Those holes in our bodies where other bodies have unabashedly entered and left their deposits. Among other things, the body's archive might be framed as an archive of penetration. A cellular recounting of sloughs of skin, of bodily fluids that have been shed or excreted into each body, into each of the body's canals. A history, in other words, of foreign bodily matter left inside us. In this sense, the vaginal archive also turns out to be an anal and oral and acoustic one... Each orifice an entry where we palpably open, where other bodies have been, and by leaving their traces in us have, in a molecular sense, become us.

This thought is at times distressing to me when I reflect upon a history of forced and unwanted bodily entry, or of those fleeting shameful affairs I have so often wished to make disappear from my archive. I do not want to retain those remnants, nor at times can I bear that to some degree, however infinitesimally, I am constituted by them. Lest I forget, though, that we also shed ourselves over time. This body is not the body it was then and is already becoming another body. This formula offers degrees of relief and panic in turn. It is also another kind of fiction. Suddenly I am aware of the body as both archive and archivist – in a crucial sense, it gathers its own materials. Control over the assemblage that I am turns out to be pure fantasy.

IN GRADUATE SCHOOL, I wrote a shoddy dissertation about representations of food and eating in postcolonial literary texts titled *The Edible Complex*. The title was its crowning achievement, and even that was given over to me by my doctoral advisor. What is important to me now about that dissertation is that it is a sign of my historical preoccupation with what enters the body and how and why. With the ways in which we take in, refuse or expunge things that are external to us. It was a novice attempt to conceive an anti-colonial archive of ingestion, with special attention to how colonial legacies continue to inform our bodies and minds.

The French gastronome Jean-Anthelme Brillat-Savarin once famously pronounced: "Dis-moi ce que tu manges, je te dirai ce que tu es" ("Tell me what you eat, I will tell you what you are"[3]). He claimed a critical relation between one's identity and one's diet, reminding us that eating habits reveal or betray so many forms of identity, including race, ethnicity, class, culture, gender. And also, perhaps, sexuality... but I will come to that.

There is a moment in an interview with Jean-Luc Nancy when Derrida insists that it is inconceivable for a head of state in the Western world to be vegetarian today. What he means by this is that the top political dog must unabashedly consume other bodies in order to be seen as an effective state leader. Eating meat becomes a sign of willingness to obliterate other beings. There's a funny perversion at work in this formulation, if you think about it. The head of state becomes a kind of cannibal: he is one whose carnivorous authority is a mirror of his capacity to willingly devour other humans.

---

3   Jean-Anthelme Brillat-Savarin, *Physiologie du goût* (Paris: Flammarion, 2001), 19.

Yet in the fantasy of Western imperial power, the cannibal is never the self but the other, those "savage" sub-human beings whose cultural practices of eating other humans makes them legitimate subjects of colonial domination. For the most part, cannibalism turns out to be a colonial invention. In his anthropological work, Claude Lévi-Strauss details the conditions under which cannibalistic practices have been ritually enacted by particular cultures at particular historical moments. Far from being savage acts of devouring other human bodies in orgiastic feasts, Lévi-Strauss shows us that cannibalistic practices tend to have deeply spiritual and often honorific valences. Rarely are they about eating a whole body, but are rather discrete, symbolic acts of incorporation. A small act of taking the body of another into yours. Whether the flesh consumed is that of the enemy or the loved one, taking in a piece of another body into yours is a way of neutralizing its power or claiming it as part of you.

Cannibalism, Lévi-Strauss provocatively suggests, is a far less brutal act than the more familiar register of life imprisonment, where the enemy's body is not taken into the body but expunged to the shackled margins of society. An enemy who today, thanks to the modern prison-industrial complex, is increasingly made to be productive to and for the state that has captured it. A permanently caged monster.

MY MOTHER IS UNDENIABLY aging, and I find myself ru-
minating over her death. I have in fact been bracing for
the end of her life since I was a child, because she has had
a long-standing habit of insisting on the immanence of
her demise. In all this time spent anticipating her end, I
have from time to time imagined taking a small piece of
her flesh into my body. I am already made up of her in
more ways than I can know, yet to have her pass through
me so palpably, to have her become part of me one last
time in this indisputable way, would hold another kind
of meaning.

This morning, while putting on her shoes and heading
off to summer camp, my daughter casually asserts that
she desires to eat me. Before the words have settled in the
air, she quickly retracts her desire, realizing that eating
me would compromise her capacity to snuggle my body.
Her father, a queerdo if ever there was one, smiles know-
ingly and says: "That's called ambivalence, my dear. "

Should I be so bold then as to claim that our mutual desire to eat our mothers is inter-generational? To add to
the strangeness of our shared desire, I submit here the
fact that my child and I are both vegetarians. We expressly avoid eating other animals. And yet we are struck by
this brazen urge, a love of the maternal body so deep as
to want to root it right inside us.

Early in his autobiography, Mohandas Gandhi confesses
to his rebellious teenage acts of meat eating. He was a fel-
low who loved his mother unabashedly and revered her
strict vegetarianism. While Gandhi was raised vegetarian, meat eating became for a short while in his youth
the antidote to overthrowing his English colonizers. Like
an Indian superhero, he imagined that he'd literally beef
himself up and throw out the Brits. He would of course
famously reverse this formulation, leaning on a vegetar-

ian ethico-politics that for him became key to refusing to be ruled by external forces. But in those early years, as he flirted with forms of colonial resistance, he secretly consumed sheep meat, and recalls in his autobiography being plagued at night by haunting bleating sounds emerging from within his sinful body.

It was never the idea of ingesting or digesting animals that steered me away from meat consumption; rather, it was the felt knowledge of meat *production* that haunted me. It was that unforgettable awareness of how animal lives are ruled over before becoming meat that stalled my capacity to eat their flesh. But my desire to eat my mother falls beyond this economy. Unlike the majority of lives consumed as meat in the Western world, and unlike those we like to indefinitely imprison, my mother has not lived her life shackled and caged. Though she undoubtedly harbors a host of her own historically motivated demons and has been psychically captured by the legacies of the Holocaust that produced her, she is essentially a free-range creature and has lived a long life of physical freedom. I could therefore consume her flesh without ethical crisis. Even with a kind of sensational relish.

MY PERSONAL HISTORY OF digestion has been an over-whelmingly disgraceful one. Historians of the body might conceptualize mine as a history of alimentary crisis: a brown girl's history of wrestling with a white girl's disorder. When Susan Bordo published *Unbearable Weight* in 1993, it gave feminists a Foucauldian frame for interpreting eating disorders as complex negotiations of the institutionalized stranglehold of modern, Western femininity. Back then, Bordo had diagnosed eating disorders as belonging to white, highly educated girls.

This was right around the time I began to find myself compulsively hunched over toilets, developing the skills of bulimic discretion that one needs in order to become "good" at the practice. There were humiliating bumps along the way to be sure, but eventually I became very skilled at the requisite methods – physical and psychological – of masking for myself and for others a literally unpalatable condition. I was a mixed-race high school kid who had all but dropped out, who was spending my days crashing on a friend's couch watching *Days of Our Lives* and *Jerry Springer* (back when he was "political," before he fashioned himself as a total wanker). A kid who had left home at fifteen, who was killing time by binging and purging, then drinking Wild Turkey straight from the bottle on an empty stomach while tucked into a sleeping bag that was menacingly covered in little holes from my cigarette ashes. I had no taste at all for alcohol or cigarettes, but I was trying to prove a point, trying to cultivate how I felt. I was someone who, in other words, was not accounted for within the discourses of bulimia circulating at that time.

In a later anniversary edition of her book, Bordo would come to revise her profile of the bulimic subject after it had become clear in the new century that eating disorders had gone global, and that white girls weren't so special anymore in the art of sickening self-mastery.

Despite my tomboyish style and demeanor, and against my own budding feminist politics, it is certainly possible that back then I wanted so badly to be a certain kind of white girl that I perfectly acted out her disease. After all, I had learned disordered eating from other girls in my family who, like me, had no outlet for thinking or feeling (much less embracing) our mixed-race identities. We were profoundly uncomfortable in our skins and we ate defiantly in the face of that discomfort. My father saw the signs of his daughters' bodily growth and worried that we would become robustly Punjabi: "Don't get fat like my sisters!" he would assert in his thick Indian accent. It was clear that his desire to keep us thin was a convoluted mix of health concern and aesthetic preference. To complicate matters, we had little frame of reference for these mythical fat sisters, since he had essentially abandoned his ties to India in an effort to become authentically Canadian. My Irish-German-Jewish mother likewise advised us that snacking would have abject consequences for our future lives: "Do you want to become the fat lady in the circus?!" she would caution ominously when we felt hungry to the point of distraction. She was white and beautiful, had even modeled in Montreal in the 1960s. And so, we took her words into our bodies and we chewed them up before we snuck into the kitchen and hid food in our cheeks and pockets like little rodents on the lam.

But this historico-filial frame for my disorder can only ever be partial, a fragment of a more complicated narrative.

In her refusal of feminist theory's antibiological stance, Elizabeth A. Wilson argues that "biology and culture are not separate, antagonist forces; that a political choice cannot be made between biological and cultural agency."[4] Wilson draws extensively on what the Hungarian psychoanalyst Sándor Ferenczi's called "the biological unconscious,"[5] turning her attention to how the mind and the gut are crucially entangled organs. She suggests that bulimia might itself be understood as a kind of bodily thinking in which "bingeing and purging are the substrata themselves attempting to question, solve, control, calculate, protect, and destroy."[6] The gut, Wilson declares, is an organ that ruminates.

The gut's mind. The mind's guts. All that puking, all that need to puke, tangled up in a disquieted gut that was speaking a mind through the expulsion of its contents. Purging to quiet itself, tangled up and at play with a likewise disquieted psyche. Perhaps the limitations of the purely psychological reading of my disorder, which could not account for my body's own stakes in my chronic purging, is precisely why it took so long to stop.

4   Elizabeth A. Wilson, *Gut Feminism* (Durham: Duke University Press, 2015), 8.
5   Sándor Ferenczi, cited in ibid., 5.
6   Ibid., 63.

PURGING AS A PRACTICE more broadly defined has always been both crucial and habitual to me. While it is in no sense easy for me to discard things, doing so produces a feeling of freedom once the deed is done. Divesting myself of tangible objects is a way of refusing the over-accumulation of psychic and material stuff. Objects have power in and of themselves, but also a power in contact with us that is collaboratively created. I find real solace in sitting with that power, feeling it, and then releasing the object to the thrift store or the recycling bin, giving it over ceremoniously to an uncertain future.

Aesthetically, this habit of purging makes me a minimalist. It is an aesthetic that emerges from a resistance to the restlessness I feel when I gather too many objects, when too many material things accumulate and surround me. But this does not mean that objects are not important to me. Every object is a narrative that is already embedded in me, and how the object came to be mine is an embodied history. In this sense, the object becomes the exterior double for what is already inside me, for the historical trace that its material emergence has left in my body. In giving over the object, in sending it away, I am really only embracing its other interior configuration. A configuration that cannot be calculated, cannot be amassed, but is enfolded in and felt by the body's archive.

bodies, objects,
trau

MY BEST CHILDHOOD FRIEND P, a rogue archivist of her own history, retains everything she cherishes. There are entirely conventional aspects of her archive comprised of old answering machine messages, photographs, love notes. But there are more perverse items too, such as the single crinkly pubic hair culled from the body of the boy with whom she lost her virginity. It has moved with her across two and a half decades of her life. It travels with her. We might even say that it has in a sense become her. At the very least, it is a material sign of a moment in which she knew with absolute certainty that her body was being opened and exposed to an outside world.

LAST WINTER, A FRIEND invited me to be a guest in her graduate seminar. She had assigned my then forthcoming book about mastery and decolonization, and I was nervous to be sharing this text that had become so intimate to me but had had very little exposure to the world. It was their last meeting of the term, and as such there was a celebratory feeling in the air. As we poured pineapple rum into plastic cups and tipped our glasses, a clever graduate student turned to me and asked candidly: "Can you discuss your book's recurring preoccupation with shit?" I was dumfounded. Not by the fact that someone would ask me so unapologetically about shit, but by the fact that despite my deep intimacy with the text I had no idea that there were any references to shit therein. The student detailed them for me one by one, showing me how I had been unconsciously accounting for shit, taking stock of the butt end of a movement into, through and out of the body.

A few months later at an NYU symposium I met K, a feminist psychoanalytic thinker. There was something about her – a wildness both bodily and psychic – that I immediately appreciated. She invited me to contribute an essay to a collection she was co-editing, and I wrote about refuse – about disposable objects and what they reveal to us about ourselves. I was thinking expressly about garbage and landfills, about the culture of consumption, yet in her editorial response to my article K wrote extensively about shit as a kind of lurking figure that wanted to emerge in my prose but was never produced. She wondered over the relation between my concern with the landfill – the unruly space of social waste – and the waste produced by and through the individual body. Yet again, I had not been thinking consciously of shit and yet there it was looming in my work....

K's role in asking me to give over shit was fascinating in so far as she was stitching the editorial to the maternal. As though I was a hesitant child who wanted but could not quite bring myself to give over my shit. Or as if the text itself was a child and she another mother waiting eagerly for it to produce its gift. In any case, I loved the intimacy. In her sign-off, K wrote: "Take my musings on shit as a sign of deep engagement with your text." I began there and then to wonder whether there is any deeper form of engagement than this.

AS I WAS FALLING in love with my trans partner, I told S about this startling discovery that shit was always lingering on the edges of my prose, and relayed that I was plotting to write about it head-on. We had talked very little in this early stage of our romance about defecation, sharing an implicit sense that a degree of bodily discretion was motivating our intense sexual desire. I had recently stumbled on a study that concluded that couples who openly discuss their bowel movements have a higher relational success rate than couples who take shit as taboo. But the study never revealed the extent of these discussions, whether the couples actually shit in front of each other and discussed the process, or whether they were simply willing to confess from time to time that they had a case of the runs. This seemed to me an important scholarly elision.

The gesture of evoking shit with S was an attempt to play with the weird difference between talking about shit conceptually and producing shit in real time. It was also a way of thinking about our sex, which was unfolding through the open accessibility of my bodily orifices and the lust-inducing limits of his. I have discovered over time that I love the inaccessibility of other bodies in sexual play. There is nothing more seductive for me than a stone lover, nothing more exciting than one who takes my body entirely but strategically limits my access to theirs in turn.

In her extended meditation on queer embodiment, Maggie Nelson relays an anxiety shared by many pregnant women over the scene of childbirth, about the repercussions of their male partners witnessing another body emerging from their vaginal canals, and the likely prospect of shitting in front of them during childbirth. How, many women wonder, could their partners find them sexually desirable after seeing their bodies produce organic matter so blatantly? I'm with Nelson, who finds this formulation confounding given how close it comes to mirroring what for some of us is most sexually satisfying – the body opening up, the body letting go. Nelson disrupts the anal taboo, insisting on her interest "in the fact that the human anus is one of the most innervated parts of the body,"[7] reminding us that the cultural unwillingness to abide by the anus sets limits on how we come to think, fuck, feel, and love.

It makes sense to me that Nelson's consideration of the anus is situated in a text that is concerned with queer and maternal embodiments. Giving birth critically recalibrated my relationship to my body, and in a real sense made me open to thinking and feeling in ways I had not thought to access before. In an obvious way, being a mother makes you open to and anticipatory about the shit of another – another whose excrement becomes part of your everyday life, part of the cont(r)act you keep making with the world.

I would be remiss here not to mention that I spring from an anally oriented family, one whose collective memories are largely constructed around scenes of shitting. The link between the maternal and the anal runs deep for me. A case in point is my mother's infamous "bolon knife," an ordinary kitchen knife she would access each time the toilet was clogged with a "bolon," her clinical term for an excessively large shit. We children would become all energy and excitement when our sibling would produce a bolon, circling wildly around our mother as she made her way to the knife drawer. As she marched up the stairs to the toilet, knife in hand, we would fall in line like a row of mesmerized ducklings, almost reverential toward her

7   Maggie Nelson, *The Argonauts* (Minneapolis: Graywolf Press, 2015), 85.

singular determination to dismember the shit beast. We would gather around the toilet to gawk collectively at the immensity of the feces, and watch our mother maim it before delivering it to its destiny, heroically flushing it away.

S was amused to learn about my preoccupation with shit (which I took as a promising sign) and immediately introduced me to Michel Gondry's short film *One Day* (2001). The film stars Gondry himself as the defecator and David Cross as his feces. It opens with Gondry emerging from a bathroom stall followed, to his discomforting surprise, by his giant humanoid feces. Looking at Gondry squarely, his feces asks: "We're not friends anymore?" After a brief chase in which Cross-as-poo publicly accuses Gondry of attempted murder-by-flushing, the feces agrees to drop his charges if Gondry will "recognize" him. Gondry hesitantly concedes and the feces affectionately declares him Papa as he embraces his maker with his shit-body. Ashamed and humiliated by his fecal offspring, a series of madcap scenes ensue until Gondry wakes up the next morning to his shit having shed its fecal body and emerged as a Nazi who controls and abuses him. In the final scene, the feces-cum-Nazi shouts: "You can run but you can't hide, Gondry! I *am* you!"

All this to say that I am not singular in my consideration of the stakes of caring for shit, though I suspect that my own maternal forms would produce quite different results from Gondry's hilariously halting and discomforted acts of fecal fathering. Perhaps what I really mean to say is that I want to be responsible to and for my body, for everything it yields.

ON A TRIP TO Cuba, my friend L failed to defecate for ten consecutive days. When her body finally evacuated itself, it was such an extraordinary event that she declared the giant feces her poo baby. There was an irony at work here, because she had been trying quite desperately for over a year to become pregnant. With pregnancy as her desired horizon, miscarriages and menstruation became signs of the body's failure, or even worse, signs of the body's betrayal. When her Cuban poo baby emerged, it was at last a marker of bodily success. Even perhaps a talisman announcing that a flesh baby might be next... Yet when L's poo baby finally came to fruition, I took seriously it's emergence and kept wondering: "What might it mean to mother it?"

It was shortly after the birth of her poo baby that L was diagnosed with Stage IV lung cancer. After a series of critical misdiagnoses, she was finally discovered to be riddled with tumors in her lungs, brain, bones, breasts... It seemed by then that no part of her had been left untouched. Before this diagnosis, she had been subjected to a medical style of reading her "type," which began with an assessment of her profile as a Type A personality – a highly successful, white academic woman. Suffering from symptoms that ranged from extreme shortness of breath to recurring hallucinatory aura migraines, she was repeatedly diagnosed with anxiety and depression as the root of her problems. She knew these diagnoses to be both correct and entirely insufficient: *of course* she was anxious and depressed, which were coherent responses to the experience of her body beginning to mysteriously interact with itself and the world in ways entirely foreign to her. She was reacting to the feeling of losing herself. The symptoms were mistaken for the cause.

In the days immediately following her terminal diagnosis, L became terrified to eat. She was staying with her partner's family in Leeds, all of them struggling to absorb the impossible fact of her imminent death. I was approaching the second trimester of my pregnancy and was still wretchedly ill with morning sickness that was most acute at night, so we skyped in the dark while everyone around us slept, plotting how to save her by putting our mutual research skills to work. L kept repeating "I'm starving, I'm starving..." But food had suddenly become a threat of feeding the disease. We needed to know more, she insisted, before we allowed anything to enter her body. Some part of me understood that the worst that could happen is that we explode another bomb in an already devastated environment, so I urged her to eat whatever was on hand. But she was determined to shield the broken thing that she was. Eating would remain a threat until the research had been done, until a plan had been hatched for a cure that would never come.

We believed for a few solid months that putting the right things into her body would enable it to restore itself. We learned about natural ways to survive terminal diagnoses. Clinics in the US that might save her organically. Mushrooms as the cure! Mushrooms as pure threat! We learned that juicing was crucial, so our girl posse pooled our scarce resources and shipped a high-end juicer across the ocean. A year later at her wake in an Irish pub in Winnipeg, L's in-laws confessed that we had bought the wrong machine for our beloved friend. The one we shipped did not pulverize sufficiently its contents and was therefore useless for curing cancer. Realizing our error, L had secretly purchased a new one. But her in-laws reported at her wake that they still used and enjoyed our machine. Last week, exactly five years after its purchase, I received an email recall notice for the machine and hit delete.

L was beautiful, compassionate, incredibly smart, charismatic. A beekeeper's daughter who when we met in our teens was the bass player in a Canadian punk band. We were the two members of our sprawling teen girl posse to become academics. And not coincidentally, we were also the two who struggled most with food and eating. After her diagnosis, she bemoaned the time wasted on those rigorous practices of bodily cultivation and control that had so governed over her, that were still then governing over me. She had become almost bone at that point and laughed critically at how sick it was that it took dying to reach that perverse feminine ideal. But a few months later, when a new course of medication bloated up her skinny frame, she confessed that she was once again deep in worry over her bodily appearance, even on the verge of death. And for a minute we laughed at how twisted we were, how abidingly fucked up.

WE CAME INTO COLLECTIVE sexual awareness during the AIDS crisis, a gaggle of Canadian girls acting tough in the face of so many vulnerabilities. AIDS seemed both remote and palpably threatening, something looming just south of the border. In the United States, AIDS was unfolding as a religious and political alibi for letting unwanted citizens die. Though in my sheltered Canadian teen world I understood it less as a state-sanctioned genocide of gay men and more as a riveting American television teen drama. I was hooked on a Sunday evening show in which the sensitive girl protagonist's heart-throb boyfriend, a bad boy with a heart of gold, had contracted the disease through shared needles. While the overt social message was clear – that "we" need not fear contact or emotional intimacy with those who test positive for HIV – it was also clear in that special Hollywood sense that some bodies afflicted were valuable, marketable, compassion-inducing. And some were not. Though the media frenzy around HIV/AIDS was blatantly pitching it as a "gay disease," it nevertheless contributed to my hesitations about sexual intercourse with men. But there were, of course, other ways of accounting for that hesitation.

In her analysis of representations of queer children, Kathryn Bond Stockton reveals that from the vantage point of adulthood, it is not the child but childhood itself that turns out to be queer. Childhood, she argues, is an adult fantasy of a time and space from which we must "grow up" straight into proper heterosexual adulthood. A fantasy, in other words, in which we can imagine ourselves as having reached a vertical form of completion. I was a queer child, then, in so far as we were all queer children. I have no narrative of "the closet" to share and understand my emergence into queer subjectivity as one that grew alongside my intellectual development. Body and mind, intellect and desire – there is no longer a way for me to frame these as discrete categories.

Back then, I was teaching myself to be tough, to revolt against signs of femininity in my desperation for grit and depth. Being a girl felt frivolous, like an embodied act of self-betrayal. At seven, I was chosen to be a flower girl in my Uncle A's wedding in Toronto. Uncle A was my mother's significantly younger brother, the age between them wide enough that they were essentially strangers. (Perhaps it bears mentioning here that he encouraged us to call him "Uncle Anus" for reasons totally mysterious to me then and now.) This was the white side of my family whom I scarcely knew, a family that had immigrated from Ireland and had been maternally inscribed by the atrocities and displacements of the Holocaust. I was entirely ambivalent about this nuptial event. I felt a degree of excitement about a family event in another, bigger city, with people we hardly knew. And I felt special to have been chosen as flower girl. But when the time came, I also felt utterly mortified as I was coaxed into a little white dress, into getting my gnawed fingernails painted, into posing for pictures in a sea of regaled whiteness in which I felt ugly and alien. I wanted out of the humiliation – out of the wedding regalia, but also out the thing I was, the monstrous thing I felt myself to be.

And then in walked Cousin K, and the world seemed to change. Cousin K was a teenage talisman whose meaning I would not decipher until decades later. There and then, I could only feel the impact of her like an impossible swell through my body. Everyone knew that Cousin K was "gay." My mother waved K's flag in our childhoods, declaring time and again that "Every Good Family Needs a Gay!" K had refused to attend the wedding in a dress and donned instead what everyone called "a peter pan outfit." (As I write this, I want to reach back into the 1980s and behold that outfit, which is no doubt now in vogue again.) But it was less the fashion that caught me and more the fact and signification of K's refusal. It was a refusal I hadn't even considered for myself, to be there on my own terms. I was enchanted by her aesthetics and her conviction. She was the super-heroic star of that wedding, my unconsciously drafted prototype of the queers I would come much later to love so fiercely.

On our last night in Toronto, Cousin K came to our hotel room to say goodbye. My family had not learned how to be intimate and did not engage in loving forms of touch, but K was at ease as she reached to embrace each one of us. When my turn came, I let myself be gathered up by her but forced my body not to cling to hers. I wanted to steal a private moment with her, to express something I had not yet developed a vocabulary for. A feeling without words. She felt like a gift, something singularly exceptional that I wanted for always and was about to lose.

When I let K go I promptly pitched a fit over my mother's refusal to let me have a candy bar from the vending machine in the hotel hallway. My mother must have been mystified by my response, since we all knew it was useless to ask for candy. I too couldn't begin to understand my own reaction – I was all feeling, all hopeless desire, yet I had no idea what for. Cousin K seemed to understand intuitively that my tears were a displacement. She said something to me I can't quite remember ("I know it's hard to say goodbye"?), some softer articulation of my feeling of absolute loss. I felt embarrassed by her words, as though she had misunderstood me completely. I was trying to become certain that my tears were not for her; I had wanted something sweet, I told myself, and that was all...

And then I watched her leave, a queer spirit I never met again.

YEARS AGO, I TOLD an academic mentor that my engagements with queer theory had produced in me an unabashedly queer sexual desire. I was caught off guard when, on theoretical grounds, he refused this formulation outright. He had a special fancy for young, brown intellectual women, so he undoubtedly had something at stake in maintaining the instability of my claim. But my desire was certainly there, and as such could not be denied. While he couldn't take seriously queer theory's palpable effects on me, what he insisted upon was the relation between my decades-long practice of vegetarianism and my desire for queer sex. To his mind, the relation was clear and could be boiled down to a commitment to what he called my alternative politics.

Queer studies had been entirely absent from my formal education, seeped as I was in continental philosophy and postcolonial studies. Suddenly, I was devouring queer texts like Skittles (obviously, you can't just stop at one). I had become especially enamored by J's thinking, whom I had dubbed without yet knowing him "the prince of queer theory." I finally met J was when I invited him to give a talk in Richmond. His work had become indispensable to my thinking, and unbeknownst to me he had just finished reviewing my academic manuscript. We shared an immediate intimacy by virtue of having dwelled in each other's thought. I took him to Church Hill for Turkish pastries, and while standing in line J narrated a scene from the British film *Pride* (2014). In the film, an aging nun turns to a group of young queers and says: "There's something I've always wanted to ask you people..." You expect the nun to ask a salacious question about queer sex, but instead she asks confoundedly: "Why are you all vegetarians?!" As an unapologetic carnivore, J found this scene hilarious. The joke works, of course, because it points to the almost predictable ways that some of us enact "alternative politics." But it's also hilarious because it nods to the entanglements of eating and sex – both acts constituted by what enters and moves through the body, and why.

EATING AND VOMITING, INVITING in and expunging, are undeniably tied through the passage they travel: the journey touches all the same corridors, simply in reverse. I became vegetarian and bulimic not quite simultaneously. (Vegetarianism came first, if this is at all important.) These movements into vegetarianism and purging were a long time coming, rooted as they were in deeper histories. They were emerging long before they surfaced. Perhaps they even predate me.

For clinicians, the relation between my vegetarianism and bulimia would make a great deal of sense, since both acts signal control over what gets consumed and digested. Yet increasingly, I see no clear distinction between these and other seemingly less controlled forms of incorporation: We are always taking in and refusing, incorporating and setting limits, on what we allow into our bodies. The same can be said for other bodily practices, for how we grow into our desires, for how we select what parts of the world we will and will not take in, for how the world passes through us.

I'm especially invested in what we allow ourselves to allow in. I'm interested in what was once a prohibition that becomes, over time, a vital and sustaining way of life.

Does it make sense, given all this, that leaning into queerness would coincide with a waning need to purge? Not that one was the root of the other. Not at all. Simply a desire that corresponded so stunningly with another desire. In each case, a need to nurture myself differently. I thought of this the other day while sitting in the grass with my daughter, solar eclipse glasses covering our eyes as we watched the moon pass between the earth and the sun, changing the tone of the world just then. An alignment that turned time and space into a strange, satisfying kind of enchantment.

The Inarticulate Trace

Extreme physical pain swallows its object. It dwarfs you. I find a certain perverse comfort in being with others who have endured indescribable pain. It is a comfort of its own order, and in this sense is almost antithetical to other forms of comfort that tend toward stability. The comfort of discovering others who share the experience of indescribable pain is, oddly, one that mirrors pain's dwarfing effect; I feel shrunken by my proximity to others who have been fundamentally altered by pain. And in the strangest sense, I relish this feeling.

Though pain is internally felt and appears to belong to discrete bodies, it is also vitally bound up with the outside world. Pain comes through an already existing body, but it is interpreted, diagnosed, and valued from the outside. Before there is an evaluation of pain, there is a suffering body. And this body is always already interpreted before pain is assessed; pain is, in other words, diagnostically secondary to the body that feels it. The more immediately "legible" forms of bodily assessment – the gender, race, class, and sexuality that are often revealed by the body – come first. Put simply, pain cannot be disassociated from the political, cultural, and historical legacies that give rise to us as particular and particularly embodied subjects.

I have been told repeatedly across my life that I am a person with a high threshold for pain. This state of being poses a crucial problem for the interpreters of pain, who rely on specific affects, sounds, expressions, and phrases to inform their diagnoses. I reveal these signs later than others do. In other words, I withhold the extent of my damage until it becomes unbearable to do so.

I have often wondered over what it means to have a "high threshold for pain." This question became a preoccupation of my childhood, a time when I briefly imagined myself to be a brown girl superhero – one who might cut herself and instantly heal, or fall from a great height and emerge unscathed. I engaged in painful experiments with my body and learned through recurring injuries that whatever "high threshold" meant, it did not mean that I was immune to injury or its felt manifestations.

Later, I came to wonder whether "high threshold" meant not that I was immune to pain but that I felt it differently from others. Yet this formulation kept falling apart, for no matter how many conversations I engaged in about pain there seemed no convincing way to measure my pain against the pain felt by others. In trying to measure the distance between the pain belonging to me and the pain of others, I came face to face with the limited vocabulary and insufficient metaphors we rely on to articulate something that, in the end, does not really have a place in language.

Eventually, I began to examine the phrase "high threshold for pain" not by circling around pain, but by turning to the term "threshold." That space – physical, psychic, and temporal – from which you can no longer sustain a performance of yourself as a discrete and bounded entity. The threshold of pain is the body's breaking point, where you move from a recognizable version of yourself to something wholly estranging.

I have a lingering and unprovable suspicion that my own threshold is not natural, not something organic to me. Rather, it grew over time, emerging through more and less subtle forms of training. Threshold is pedagogy. When I feel pain, I hush it up and keep my head high. I push the threshold into a distance, so that it becomes a thin line that tests my endurance, as though I am medal-worthy for my capacity not to succumb to it.

MY LIFE WITH ACUTE neurological pain is now several years past, yet it haunts unlike other ghosts I have known. It is not quite the memory of pain I am pointing to, though the memory is always near. It is as though the experience of pain produced another body that trails after mine, close at hand but spectral. Those urgent, intolerable sensations have subsided, yet my body is undeniably changed by the pain it suffered. I live, as a physical and emotional being, very differently in its aftermath.

After a year of abiding and intensifying pain I underwent a precarious emergency neurosurgery and entered thereafter into the phase called recovery. Throughout this period – through post-surgical visits and therapies both physical and psychological – it became increasingly clear that recovery was a kind of assuaging fiction. Before my life with pain, I had been living a fiction of my body as a stable thing – a thing that would remain intact simply because I couldn't imagine life otherwise. In recovery, movement became not freedom but threat. Everyday life produced a kind of terror in which every motion signaled the possibility of irreparable damage. In pain, something had been uncovered that could not be covered over again.

In her memoir *A Body, Undone*, Christina Crosby writes the bewilderment of her life with quadriplegia. The memoir shuttles back and forth between life before and after her cycling accident; between memories of her own body and the bodies of others; between an embodied life full of pleasurable sensations, and a life that has become nearly unlivable. Pushing against a tendency within a discourse that advocates for the embrace of differently-abled bodies, Crosby insists on writing about her refusal to find optimism in the intolerable nature of her pain. For her, there are crucial stakes in not pretending to embrace something that swallows your life.

When my Queer Lit students read Crosby's memoir last year on the heels of Donald Trump's presidential inauguration, a student I especially love raised her hand and asked: "Aren't we all differently abled, in the end? Shouldn't we be in radical embrace of different experiences of the body? And doesn't Crosby's memoir, in her nostalgia for her life before quadriplegia, become weirdly ableist?"

My response to this question was not verbal but bodily. I felt a shock of nerve pain run from my lower back through to the base of my foot. I heard the piercing echo of that unbelievable recurring cry that I had made in pain. I became physically struck before all of those keen, critical young faces. I looked at my beloved student and thought through my body: "Can we put aside our training in political correctness and let pain, that inarticulate beast, sound its impossible noise? Can we listen together differently?"

For all of the ways that I remain bound to pain, I can find almost nothing to say about its specificity. When I first tried to write about extreme physical pain, I discovered that I could only write in opaque poetic fragments. Pain seemed to belong more to poetry than to narrative prose. But even poetry, for all of its subtle rendering, fails to capture the *pain* of pain, its illegible core.

Elaine Scarry writes that "physical pain does not simply resist language, but actively destroys it, bringing about an immediate reversion to a state anterior to language, to sounds and cries a human being makes before language is learned."[1] For Scarry, pain obliterates language, returning us to pre-linguistic forms of expression, to a time and

1   Elaine Scarry, *The Body in Pain: The Making and Unmaking of the World* (New York & Oxford: Oxford University Press, 1985), 4.

place we cannot remember but that was witnessed by others. Scarry wonders over where language is in pain, and where pain is in language.

The onset of my inarticulate pain occurred in close proximity to the birth of my only child, and it grew alongside her over the course of almost a year. In both childbirth and neurological pain, I became a human whose language was utterly lost to extreme sensation. And in both contexts, I not only *felt* but *heard* myself become other than myself, other *to* myself. Yet remembering Scarry, my "immediate reversion to a state anterior to language" was entirely unlike sounds I had ever heard other humans make. They were not pre-linguistic human sounds, but post-linguistic alien echoes. In each instance I became alien to what I had known myself to be, a different kind of creature altogether. Yet if these were in some perverse sense twinned experiences, they were also each singularly unique. Each made me manifest as a different kind of unrecognizable being, each produced me as a different kind of creaturely thing. One experience I can imagine returning to with an intense flourish; the other I fear I would not survive again.

I WAS INTENSELY QUIET throughout my 24-hour labor until I began at the tail end to utter mythical, feral moans. In labor, I fell into a deep, meditative space that I could not have anticipated. In that long quietude, my queer best friend and co-parent, N, tried maniacally to track my contractions on a phone app he had been told was "indispensable" to modern labor. I was somewhere between unwilling and unable to narrate the beginnings and ends of my body's contractions. N, desiring to be the best "birthing partner" he could be, was left speculatively finger tapping his phone, asking repeatedly "was that one?!" without ever receiving a response.

Quietude came to an end at that point where there was no longer ambiguity over whether or not I would speak: I was another thing altogether – somewhere beyond language where you become only body and body; yours and that of the intimate stranger you are producing. This state of body and body was sonically alien, a rhythmic repetition of otherworldly moans. N, who studies musical sound, had by then abandoned his phone and was acoustically enraptured, never before having listened so intently.

We were unprepared for childbirth. N and I had felt bored and amusingly infantilized in childbirth classes, which we quickly abandoned. We were baffled when we were asked to engage in "the ice cube exercise," where we were made to hold an ice cube in our hands until we could no longer tolerate it. What was the point of this exercise? It is meant to mimic the intensity of a contraction but fails in so many directions. We learned nothing about the sensation of childbirth from this exercise, nothing about the particular intensities or temporalities of a contraction, nor my capacity to endure one. We couldn't glean anything from this pedagogy, so we dropped out like wayward stoners.

Meanwhile, I found myself feeling persistently enraged by the language, tone, and form of almost every birthing book that friends sent my way. Rather than playing with ice cubes and indulging in ideologically suspect literature, N proposed that to prepare for the inevitable birth of our child we study documentary footage of mammals giving birth. Watching mammalian birthing footage was instructive on several counts, not least of which was the sonic dimension of animal labor. Set against a long history of television and Hollywood film representations of high-pitched screaming women rushed on gurneys through hospital hallways, the sounds of other mammals were of entirely different tenors and tones.

I have been compelled by the sonic life of pain ever since I birthed my child, compelled by the ways that producing painful sounds resonates into futures well beyond the utterance. That mythical moan, that human-animal-alien sound of body giving over body, was generative in a definitional sense. It was the sound of production, of making something other than oneself and making oneself as other.

I still wonder over how different our births and lives would be if we were not so rigidly trained into gendered forms of articulation. If instead of the high-pitched screaming of pop culture's singular representation of childbirth, we could create access to other forms of necessary, embodied noise-making. A genre and gender shattering sound archive.

ROBIN COSTE LEWIS'S POEM "On the Road to Sri Bhu-vaneshwari" turns on the body and things expunged from it. In the poem, a group of American students traveling to a temple in the Himalayan foothills are detained on the road as a buffalo gives birth. Amidst so many bodies – foreign students, nomadic herders, her own animal clan – the buffalo mother births a stillborn calf, "a folded and wet black nothing."[2] Having expunged the stillborn she tries to bolt, tries to leave that painful thing behind her. The herders surround and detain the buffalo mother, believing that she must confront the "black nothing" so as not to go mad. "They wait through her heaving. They sing / to her, they coo. Men who are midwives." In response to the buffalo's pain – corporeal and psychic – the herding men sing and coo songs as a passage, as a sonic balm that will help her to face (in the most literal sense) her trauma: "Finally, after half an hour / of bucking and grunting, she drops her eyes / and gives. She lowers her face into it – into the black/ slick dead thing folded on the ground – / and sniffs. Nudges the body. Snorts." Only then can the bereft buffalo mother disappear back into the heard, leaving behind her "slick dead thing."

Later in the poem we learn that the poet too has given birth, but to a living thing. At the poem's end she and her child face a precipice, a radical break into an uncertain future. Like the buffalo, the poet has bolted too quickly from a history that leaves her unreconciled. She writes: "I have to go back / to that wet black thing / dead in the road. I have to turn around. / I must put my face in it." Each time I read this poem, I become a herder with an aim to detain this poet-beast, to grip her until she stills. Each time, I want to coo to her until she drops her head.

2 Robin Coste Lewis, "On the Road to Sri Bhuvaneshwari," in *Voyage of the Sable Venus and Other Poems* (New York: Alfred A. Knopf, 2015), 6–14.

Each time, I want to sing to that unbearable past, which also turns out to be the soundtrack to an open and more beautiful future.

WHEN A RELIGIOUSLY MINDED friend and I became simultaneously pregnant, she sent me a book written by a French male pediatrician. I can no longer recall its title or its author, though it remains with me as an object-idea that I have discarded but that lingers in my body. It was the strangest book written with the greatest conviction, part speculative meditation from the position of the child being born, part philosophical treatise, and part photographic evidence of the child's alleged birthing trauma. Among the pediatrician's central claims was that the modern hospital room is a space that inflicts unnecessary violence upon the newborn child. The bright lights, the surgical instruments, the noise of the room all produce an excessive shock for the child in its emergence into the world. What the pediatrician ultimately desired was a reform of the practices and environments into which many children are born.

I could easily get behind that affective and spatial critique of modern birthing practices. But what jarred me was his more foundational claim. He argued that birth itself was an act of great violence inflicted from the very first onto the child. For him, the passage through the mother's vaginal canal was itself primordially traumatic. The mother's body, he suggested, is invariably the first violence to affront the child. Because of this inevitable violence, he argued, we must make the space into which the child emerges a gentler one.

On the verge of giving birth, how was I to sit with this notion – so utterly patriarchal – that the maternal body is an inescapable site of trauma? Could he have been serious? (Indeed, in that particularly French philosophical way, he could not have been more serious.)

I knew that my vagina was considered through phallocentric logic a zone of violability, historically and politically a site of desired or requisite conquest. The vagina remains, almost ubiquitously, a place of experienced or anticipated trauma. I had gleaned through early undergraduate feminist study that the vagina, in all of its "hidden mystery," poses an imagined threat to the penis, a threat best illustrated through the folklorish figure of the *vagina dentata*, a toothed vagina that is hungry to devour the organ that enters into it. I had, in other words, considered with humor the emasculating threat that the vagina posed to a phallic outside wanting in. Yet I had never really considered its flipside, an evocation of the vagina as a space somehow organically designed to traumatize that which passes through it from within. The pediatrician's imagination of childbirth took the *vagina dentata* and inverted it, making every act of inaugural exit from the female body an act of radical trauma.

While Gandhi's gender politics were limp at best, I remain compelled by his formulation that there is no life without violence. For him, life itself necessitates violence, even if at the molecular level. We must eat to live, we must breath, we must make sanitary spaces in which to thrive, and thus we must do harm to other forms of life in order to sustain our own. I am therefore willing to concede that in so far as *everything* is linked to violence, birth must also have a relation to it. Yet in my own experience of childbirth, under a gleaming supermoon in the earliest hours of that spring morning as my body was opening wider than it ever had before, violence felt entirely elsewhere. We were one body preparing to make ourselves two, and the world was all flesh and feeling, body giving body. I went so deep into the thing I am that I couldn't open my eyes, couldn't let the outside world in even while I was so unabashedly giving something over to it.

But a violent trauma inflicted on the child? She moved through my body, collaborating to make space for herself where there had been no space before. It was an enact-ment of real and consequential agency-making, of work-ing collectively to become ourselves differently.

I have never understood the nature of my friend's strange gift. I wondered what she had found in that book that was for her worth holding and giving over. Did she be-stow it because she too found the absurdity in it? I doubt-ed this, if only because she tended toward austerity. I was pondering how to pay thanks for such an object, how to acknowledge graciously a gift that offends. A gift that keeps returning long after it is cast off.

DAYS AFTER GIVING BIRTH, my terminally ill friend L called from overseas and asked me to narrate the experience of childbirth. It was a pointedly challenging moment for us both, wanting to share in each other's lives, though it was undeniably painful for both of us to do so. Wanting to stay real with her, I said: "I meditated until I moaned; I made and simultaneously became a new animal." She was unfailingly gracious and responded that she had been immersing herself in readings about the practice of meditating into death. She said she wished for a meditation that would lead her into her last, surrendering sound. Then she disconnected quickly to avoid saying the words she also felt: "Yours is the moan that I wanted, the moan that my body will not make." Listening to the sound of emptiness at the end of our call, I wanted nothing more than to give her my moan; I wanted to offer over a sound-gift that made life, that might in some magical way sustain hers.

The feral moan of childbirth was a fundamentally altering sound. The sonic life of that radical transformation continued to resound in my life as the mother I was becoming (and am still becoming). That sound produced for me a version of myself entirely unknown to me until I was making it. As though the utterance itself was shaping me anew. That sound came to inform my whole sense of the relational world I had re-entered from another vantage point. Those alien moans were focus, determination, desperation, promise, and pain in turns. Their multivalence came to mirror my experience of motherhood's widest emotional range – from bliss to despair and all that exists in between. The generative alien moan of labor informed my motherly self, a deep sonic life-core that has always been there but that one discovers with absolute surprise.

IN THE MONTHS AFTER childbirth, I began to utter other entirely unrecognizable sounds. Other sounds. Less moan, more crippling wail that seemed to live without end. It took time to get there, to degenerate to that point where no one – not even I, a great bearer of pain – was capable of pretending that the threshold had not been far surpassed. By then, I was deep in pain. Descending into it until the idea of myself, the thing I had known myself to be, began to disappear. What was I becoming, this thing that was indistinguishable from pain? I was becoming pain itself, becoming what was both unbearably foreign and produced most intimately from within my own body.

Before the absolute break, I sought help so variously it became a kind of second career. It had never occurred to me that the pain I was enduring would not abate without radical intervention. I somehow imagined that because I had not suffered an injury inflicted by the outside, my body would heal itself with the proper regimen over time. So, I fell into the hands of a wellness center in my new city, where I gave myself over to chiropractors, massage therapists, and acupuncturists who took up my body enthusiastically in their turns.

I was financially strapped, saddled with student debt and just at the start of my life as a steadily employed person. As the child of immigrants, it had been instilled in me that debt was the very worst form of accrual, and that if you were foolish enough to have become indebted (and I was), paying it off promptly and saving 10% of every paycheck you ever earned was part and parcel of having a stable life. I was indeed paying off my debts like a ritual ablution, but any savings I might have stowed away were being given over to the wellness center, where the promise of my recovery was imbedded in the repeated expert conviction that if I only exercised more, copped more pigeon pose, increased my chiropractic sessions, did more frequent acupuncture, I would heal. Following this logic, when every form of therapy I was juggling failed to help, I was persuaded to increase the sessions, plummeting headlong into credit card debt. I was desperate to be better, driving myself as hard as the so-called experts advised, doing anything and everything to return to what I had been before. Pouring my heart, my body, and my dollars into a wellness abyss.

My chiropractor was a man who took the liberty of being wildly overfamiliar with his patients. Often, as he praised me for how well my body gave way to adjustments, he would insist that surgical intervention was for those who don't work hard enough at bodily health. When I expressed my desperation to be out of pain, my despair over seeing him constantly without feeling any results, he advised me to relieve the stress of early motherhood, to "leave the laundry unfolded" – as though the acute neurological pain that shot through my body like lightening was nothing other than the symptom of postpartum unease. "Breathe into the universe of your pain," he said with bald, bloated self-satisfaction. He never once suggested that medical intervention might be necessary, never acknowledged that the extent of my damage was lightyears beyond his capacity to heal it.

Is it okay to admit that still now, years later, I struggle against a vengeful desire to breathe pain into his universe? To dismantle every inch of that discursive and physical space?

MY PAIN INCREASED EXPONENTIALLY and became less bounded, taking on an outward sonic dimension. Just as my body could no longer contain the pain, spilling it out through sound, my daughter was increasingly chattering at the outside world. Every utterance she made hailed a kind of stunning promise of the future, the sounds of suturing herself to the world, while my sounds echoed a radical unraveling, the sound of unbecoming. We were perversely twinned and inverted, both creatures expressing what we did not have the language to speak.

I had an intensely amorous response to nearly every one of I's sounds, though the sound of her cry was unbearable and set my body into discomforting motion. Her cry produced in me a feeling of absolute and excessive suffering. This was as psychic as it was physical; I would do anything to quiet that noise. And for the first time in my life, the sound of my own cry was becoming unbearable too. I had a history of listening to the sound of my own crying, the particular sound of difficult emotional release. The sound of the sob, a sound both foreign and intimate. In an odd way, I had admired this sound.

But my neurological sounding was too extreme to be relished, too far outside what I thought I was to be sonically mesmerizing. Pain became a colonizing language that I was made to speak against every ounce of my desire and will. By the time I was hospitalized, I spoke no language other than pain. I had become nothing other than shocking sensation and immutable wail.

Over the first eight months of I's life, I had spent no more than a few hours at a time away from her. She had outright refused a bottle, insisting on my breasts as the sole source of her early sustenance, and I was thus tethered to her in ways that produced both pleasure (she needs me!) and panic (she needs me!). Among the traumatic

aspects of my galloping decent into pain was the terrifying specter of losing my capacity to mother her. Before
I was rushed into emergency surgery, I had already lost
the ability to move comfortably with her, to hold her, to
put her into her crib without experiencing intolerable
searing sensations. The pain became so consuming that
I began to faint in the face of it, dropping suddenly into
unconsciousness. It was, by that point, no longer safe to
be alone with my child.

In pain, I had also in a sense returned to being a child,
needing my own parents to tell me that I would be whole
again, would resemble myself in the future. Needing my
best friend to solo parent not only our child, but also the
helpless thing I had become.

Dr. W had been away on a family vacation over spring
break when my body broke completely. When she returned and heard the sound of my voice over the phone,
she declared that she would move mountains to arrange
an emergency MRI. It was my sound that spoke to her, that
told her what I could not say in words. Eleven months
earlier, a midwife had also diagnosed my body by sound.
As I labored from home, she listened by phone to assess
when I should deliver myself to the hospital. The echo of
these events left me wondering what women committed
to the body hear, what kind of listening makes and saves
lives.

A few hours later, when Dr. W received the MRI results,
they were so brazenly revealing that she bolted up three
flights of stairs with the scans in hand, bursting into the
neurosurgeon's office to show him the unbelievable image. Knowing that I tended toward "natural remedies,"
they quickly decided to send the scans to my medically
literate family in Canada. Witnessing the extent of my
damage, my father, a man not prone to public tears, made

a choking sound over the phone as he tried to mute his parental pain. Stifling his cries, refusing to concede to his own deepest worry, he made promises that I so desperately needed to hear: "You can be healed," and "I am traveling to you." We disconnected, and I was rushed into surgery.

MY MEMORY OF THE hospital is a narcotic remembering: the precision of some details, the surreal murkiness
of others – that unbelievable dream world from within
which there seems no other world at all. I remember wak-
ing up hazily to a stranger mechanically extracting milk
from my breasts. "We didn't want you to explode," she
said with a sympathetic smile. And I thought: "Haven't
I already exploded? Isn't this precisely why I am here?"

I remember the sudden presence of my surgeon, a man
I had never met before. I remember nothing of what he
said, but I remember his affect, the way he instilled con-
fidence in the face of precariousness. I remember thinking of him as an indispensable stranger. I wondered if he
understood how crucial it was that he not slip up, that
his surgical hands remain as steady as they had ever been
inside me. I remember trying to find a language through
which to express this.

I remember most acutely the sound of a woman in a
room beyond mine who could not contain her pain. She
screamed throughout the night, testing the patience of
our nurses. I must have inquired over her, wondered over
her pain, because I remember a nurse telling me with a
degree of intolerance that there was no medical cause
for her screaming. I wanted to say: "There are so many
forms of pain, some we find evidence for and deem ac-
ceptable, and others we refuse because we cannot understand them." That woman, a patient I never met or saw
but only heard, has stayed enduringly proximate to me. I
can say with ease that I love her. She has grown into me
and become over time a part of my body, an acoustic echo
in my sound archive.

After surgery, time took on another dimension. I remember waiting for N, my most intimate friend, who had not
yet seen me in the hospital and who had been left alone

to care for our suddenly motherless infant. He was imagining what each of our lives would become if the surgery was not successful, if the injury was too severe or if surgeon's hand slipped and I were to become suddenly paralyzed. And I remember waiting for my father, staring at the clock on the wall and wondering how much longer he might take to reach my side.

N appeared at my bedside sometime later, after the medical team had assessed my mobility, once they had deemed the surgery a success. Entering the post-operative ward, N's job was as direct and cutting as the surgeon's had been in the operating room. Enter quickly and efficiently, do what must be done. He came in alone, with a team of medical professionals waiting in quiet anticipation just outside the door. Entirely beside himself, N sat beside me and without mincing his words he said: "I love you. Your father is dead."

What sound did I make then? Can anyone remember?

MY FATHER DIED TWICE, both times in a hotel room in Fargo. He had crossed the border from Canada in pursuit of me, an act of rescue that was entirely unprecedented in our shared history. He understood the severity of my crisis and had left Canada as he had once long ago left India as an immigrant – through an act of determined urgency.

When he and my stepmother crossed the border in North Dakota, he was asked the reason for his travel. He told the customs officer that he was going to see his daughter. When asked the reason for my being in the United States, he replied that I was employed as an English professor in Virginia. As was always the case, this answer thoroughly mystified the customs officer, who struggled to understand how a brown man with an Indian accent could produce offspring that specialized in the English language. My father was detained for further questioning.

As they pulled away from the border, my father laughed at the blatant ignorance of the guards of our nations. At dinner in Fargo, he told his wife that the air was bad in the restaurant and that he needed to return to the hotel for rest. Almost as soon as he reclined on the hotel room bed, he made a single gasping sound and was gone. My stepmother screamed, utterly unprepared to lose this man she loved so unabashedly, a man who had betrayed no signs of ill health. The paramedics worked on his lifeless body while my stepmother stood stunned, thinking how extraordinary it was that even with paramedics overtaking his body on a hotel room floor in North Dakota, my father appeared so unfalteringly dignified.

And then – like a scene in a film that seems too much, too convenient, too unrealistic – he sprung back to life. And with that unfaltering dignity he scolded the paramedics, insisted that he had simply been "in a deep sleep," told them that he was a doctor and kicked them out of his room. (In fact, he was an allergist and years into retirement, but he was making a strong case for himself, assuming authority.)

Why did my father not surrender himself to the hospital in Fargo, having so clearly suffered a monumental heart attack? Months later, my stepmother told me that she believed that he simply couldn't give himself over because doing so would mean he could not board the plane to Virginia to be with me. She said this without a hint of blame, in the voice of someone willing to fill in what was not said but deeply felt. And I knew what she said to be true.

My stepmother was understandably hysterical after the paramedics hesitantly departed. She begged my father to heed their insistence that he be immediately admitted to the hospital, emphasizing the magnitude of the fact that he had just died and somehow returned to life right before their eyes. He remained stoic, comforting and calming her, telling her that if he was in danger he would go willingly to the hospital. Then he brushed his teeth, adjusted the temperature in the hotel room, climbed back into that bed beside her, held her hand and told her that she was the love of his life. And he closed his eyes, uttered once again that single gasping sound, and this time did not return.

This sound, twice uttered from my father's body, twice announcing his end, is an entirely imagined auditory event in my archive. The sound his body made when it suffered a massive heart attack – a sound that pronounced its end, and then repeated itself. Not an unwilling sound, not even resistant: a declarative sound. That I never actually heard that sound makes it no less real to me, no less part of the compilation of materials, affects, and noises that make my embodied life what it is.

At the moment of his death, his strongest desire was to produce for me the feeling that my world had not exploded and to make this feeling manifest for me. This desire in him turned out to be deeper than his willingness for self-preservation, deeper than his body-mind's capacity to sustain itself.

When he died, we were both in a foreign country, in foreign rooms with medical teams working swiftly and simultaneously on our long brown bodies. Perhaps we were becoming the same uncanny thing. Out of these strange temporally twinned medical interventions, an anticipated memory rooted itself inside me. Though he never arrived in Richmond, never came to my bedside, never cared for me as he had promised to do, the memory of all of this is as deeply embedded as historical fact. I can see him on a super-8 reel that hiccups gorgeously through my mind, cooking *cholé* and *saag* in my apartment kitchen, changing my daughter's nappies, tending to my incisions. Acts that were so unlike him, acts that he had never undertaken in our history, but that he had promised and tried into his death to fulfill. Now, his promises have become crystalized as fact, acts that never occurred but are no less essential to my impossible archive.

Other Women

I have fallen in love with someone far away, someone whose physical distance is unbearable to me. To a significant degree our relationship is unfolding in the virtual realm. I am one for whom distance is structurally painful, but I discover that it is the distance of the postmodern age that I find particularly agonizing. S and I communicate overwhelmingly through text messaging, a fundamentally tricky mode that keeps my love object feeling close at hand but fails over and again to make him fully manifest.

A friend of mine, an artist devoted to the figure of the other woman, insists that her virtual relationships — those that have taken place entirely or predominantly through technological devices — have been no less felt, no less erotic, no less powerful in their emergence or devastating in their unraveling. In other words, no less real. She tells me that in fact the deepest forms of attachment she has had are the ones that have been exclusively virtual. She thrives in that realm; for her, it is artful.

Yet for me, virtual relations feel excruciatingly remote and leave me anchorless. What I desire in the physical absence of my love is to gather and hold our correspondence — to feel it as a substantial body. My imagination of long-distance love conjures expansive exchanges of words on paper, letters carried across time and space, an archive of confessions and meditations to comb through. This imagination is partly informed by 19th-century literary depictions of love unfolding at a distance, and partly generational, since my idea of love was cultivated before the digital age.

I am often struck by a desire to return to the beginning of this love, to those first textual missives between us that mark the site of our inaugural contact. But I would have to scroll forever to reach them. I have a suspicion that even if I were to spend that endless time jutting my thumb up the screen to go back and back and back in time, my iPhone would refuse to permit me into that virtual past. Has this device archived my romance, or imprisoned it?

I ENTERED THE CELLULAR age in 2008 when my vaginal library friend C was about to give birth and wanted me on call for the immanent event. I procured a small grey flip phone that stayed with me for five years, until I stumbled into a duplicitous affair with the Love Addict. The Love Addict was in a long-term live-in relationship, one she presented as "in transition" from romance into friendship. She adored my flip phone – it may well have been what attracted her to me in the first place – but the fact that our relationship was compulsively textual meant that neither my device nor my phone plan could handle the bewildering form and frequency of our secret communications.

I therefore joined the international iPhone community in the form of the other woman, the object crashing into my life as a symbol of my need, my lack, and my capacity to deceive myself and others. It turned out that the Love Addict had a host of other women likewise tethered to their phones, vying for her to make their devices come alive. When my iPhone suddenly stopped relaying her unabashed affections, the device became a palpable symbol of my romantic annihilation.

Shortly after the end of that affair, I inadvertently let the iPhone slip from my back pocket into the toilet where it died a prompt and befitting death-by-urine. To my surprise, the new iPhone – a less expensive model that looked palpably different and felt infinitely less sleek – remained haunted by a feeling of ubiquitous lack and deception. As though the concept of the iPhone itself had a hand in making duplicity manifest.

Many moons later when I fell wildly in love with S, my iPhone continued to feel like a conduit for my idiocy, a messenger I relied on fully but also desired to annihilate. A tool that made me feel disappeared.

I WAIT (OFTEN DESPERATELY) for the *ding* of my iPhone, for the sonic register that, only an instant earlier, S was thinking of me. I know that this is a biochemical desire, that I am as addicted to the sound of his attention as I am to his attention itself. At times it becomes difficult for me to decipher the difference between them. In the instant of the text receipt, aware of the tiny temporal gap between his sending and my receiving, I can't help but to wonder: "Am I still the thing he is thinking, or has he moved on by now to other thoughts?" The fast pace of the transmission feels like a commentary on the fleet-ingness of his devotion, as though the form is revealing something suspect about the content and its sender.

I lack technological savvyness, which gives me pride and frustration in turns. Among the troubles of love unfold-ing virtually, at a distance, and primarily through screen interplay, is the fact that I am not well versed in this dia-lect. Perhaps the trouble is less that I am technologically inept, and more that I am a close-reader of language. Through many years of formal academic training and an unrelenting desire for depth, I look for nuance in eve-rything I read. And text messaging, for all of its utility and playfulness, is not an emotionally subtle genre even while it is replete with codes.

Among other tricks, I learn the "love reaction" from S, and begin to employ it regularly. When S "loves" one of my texts, a pink heart appears hovering over the top left corner of my missive. I discover innovatively that in turn I can love his love reaction, creating overlapping hearts that look like they are forming an architecture. But there is a limit to this love: the iPhone does not permit me to love the loved love. In fact, if I attempt to build upon this love by tapping on our overlapping hearts, my original heart will vanish as though I had never loved at all. While

I am not committed to the love reaction as a form, I am deeply bothered by its functional limits and effacements.

Despite its sweetness and play, the love reaction also feels to me each time I receive it like both a romantic gesture and a personal slight – a doubled shorthand that says: "Yes, yes, I love what you offer" and "I'm sorry, but I will not give over my words." This mirrors the private drama that unfolds in me each time I send a text message and receive an emoji response. If I reply to an emoji with language, I fear that I am offering too much, and if I reply with a counter-emoji, I feel that I am succumbing to a childish impulse to prove that I don't care. I discover that I never feel more vulnerable, more desperate, than when S sends me an emoji and I reply in words, and then wait for the future...

I adore S, the strange energetic being that he is. I marvel at how he can come apart and back together again without an enduring sense of shame. I am politically drawn to his embrace of messiness, his capacity to hold open so many futures at once. Yet for all of the ways I feel tied to him, I repeatedly lose him in text. I lose him, again and again, to a form of correspondence that I am now utterly addicted to, but find at once so little satisfaction in. The iPhone is a romantic set-up, a confirmation of my suspicion in the virtual. I want another language practice with him, one I can fall in love with infinitely.

Instead, because we live far apart in this technological age, and because our lives are filled with other things, we trade back and forth in a host of now familiar signs that fly through space to articulate us: a firecracker, a shining golden star, a unicorn head, a bear face, red lipstick lips, a rainbow, a swirly lollipop, a brown hand giving a thumbs-up, a glittering pink heart (and multiple other heart variations), a guy on the run, a smiling face with red hearts for eyes, a dartboard bullseye...

I FIRST MET S at a restaurant in Manhattan, an impromp-
tu event orchestrated by J, the prince of queer theory, and
his partner, M. I was in New York for a psychoanalysis
conference and, in an uncanny twist, had spent part of
my day in an Airbnb on Bleeker writing about an artis-
tic work S had made in the late nineties. I knew nothing
about S beyond this particular work, which was in a sense
from another lifetime. But the whimsical spirit of that
work was ever-present in our first encounter.

Over dinner, S described a new virtual reality collabora-
tion he was embarking on. Knowing little of virtual reality, I intuitively hedged toward suspicion. M declared that
she had been to a VR exhibit in which she observed someone getting their head smashed in, and after suffering
from nightmares she regretted the experience. J brazenly
refused the idea that the virtual had a privileged role in
producing empathy. But S had just come from a transformative VR exhibit in Brooklyn, where he had entered
the virtual world of a tree. Donning the VR headgear, he
had become tree, experiencing the branches that extended out from him, observing the creatures that made hab-
itats on his body. And then he became suddenly aware
of the threat of being chopped down. He could hear the
sounds of the chainsaw and could smell its threatening
smoke. It was a palpably haunting experience as his tree
body came under siege, as he was made into log. "Did it
hurt," I asked? I wanted to know already how real the virtual could get.

As the orchestrator of this queer match, J managed to
turn our dinner date into a mission to Big Gay Ice Cream
followed by a spontaneous trip to the theater to see Kate
Bornstein's "On Men, Women, and the Rest of Us." S sat
next to me, and as the lights went down an electric cur-
rent began to bounce between our bodies as we edged
cautiously toward each other and then apart again. I was

mesmerized by this obvious metaphor of sexual attraction coming to life, by the literal feeling of energy being produced and moving between us. For so many reasons I couldn't yet metabolize, I felt stricken when the lights went up.

After the show we bid farewell to J & M and I watched them dissolve into the city, their butch-femme magnetism leaving dynamic flecks on the pavement, the buildings, the strangers who passed them by without notice. We lingered outside La MaMa with other theater-goers until S invited me to breakfast the following day. He couldn't quite conceal his disappointment when I told him I was leaving New York early in the morning. We walked toward the subway arm bumping arm, chaperoned by S's friend who was all energy and enthusiasm but oblivious to our spark.

We were deep in conversation about the weird fantasy lives of children. S told me that his godson had expressed interest as a young child in opening up a body "to let the fun stuff spill out." As though the body was nothing other than a receptacle of joy waiting to be unleashed for the world. When we reached the subway, I was relaying the talk I had given earlier that day to a room full of psychoanalysts which had entailed narrating my childhood habit of studying my mother's sullied maxi pads. It was, admittedly, a strange note to leave on. We embraced, and I wandered toward Bleeker with a fast heart wondering why I was so quick to reveal my acute weirdness.

A few minutes later from underground, S launched what would become an elaborate, enduring, and quickly seductive virtual exchange. By morning, we were flirting with the idea of him escorting me on the 6-hour train ride back to Virginia. He asked me to send him my writing via email, a mix of academic prose and creative work. The following day, he reciprocated with word files and links to his own work. We acknowledged the thrill and fear of this mutual act, as though we were cutting ourselves open for each other in the keen, childish hope of "letting the fun stuff spill out."

Two days into our text exchange S invited me to relay my sexual desires and rendered me increasingly desperate with the promise of their fulfilment. Our magical date night had unfolded entirely in the company of friends and we had not yet spent a moment alone. In the two weeks before I saw him again, anticipating a more private encounter, I hardly ate or slept; I was losing my capacity to think beyond sexual terms. Text, it turned out, was the perfect mode for this – for the disembodied production of undeniable bodily want. And magically, it delivered on precisely what it set up. Every one of S's promises were made manifest, every one plucked out of text and made material. My body under this orchestration – the movement between the virtual and the embodied – was a days-long rotation of thirst and spill, thirst and spill.

BECAUSE S EXISTS ON social media – a time-space almost entirely foreign to me – early romantic stalking was made easy. Scrolling backwards, I discovered a whole host of images of him on Instagram, often in the company of glamorous women. Digging through his media archive, I surmised that the women in S's world appeared more woman than I had every felt myself to be. How was I to situate myself in relation to these frames? Or rather, how was I to negotiate feeling altogether alien to them? I had no orientation amidst all this feminine glamor, and my bewilderment produced a desire for flight. I had nothing womanly to offer, only words and feelings that kept spilling out of me.

A lunch date with my longtime friend A and his no-nonsense queer demeanor stalled my madness. He unabashedly refused to allow me to Instagram-stalk in his presence, insisting on his singular interest in unfiltered me. He has always held an excessively generous vision of me, and seemed thoroughly aghast that I would stoop to undermining myself through self-subjection to highly curated social media representations.

Still, I was feeling profoundly uneasy about this thing called "woman." Despite having birthed a child and professing feminist theory, I have yet to know what a woman is. And this nebulous thing remains a preoccupation.

I begin to think that there is no woman without the other woman – including the other woman that I am. Two figures that are also one, and also infinitely plural. She is an incalculable catalogue of traces that make up the body-self. Her accretions are infinite; I feel her, and I cannot stop from turning toward her.

ACROSS A LONG SUCCESSFUL haul as a butch and later as a trans guy, S has accrued a romantic history made up of women I have never met. I think about them, and from narrative scraps I conjure up their personalities, the way they live and feel their lives. I have considered their bodies, summoned the ways S has entered them, ways that are similar to or different from the ways he enters mine. I have bestowed these women with personalities that are unique and abidingly irresistible; I have crafted each of them into extraordinary being. Each one is unforgettable in her giftedness, in her generosity, in her sensitivity to the world.

At times she feels in excess of me, becomes more visible to me than I am to myself. This is not altogether surprising given my long-standing struggle with visibility. In my teens, I thought myself to be literally less perceptible than others. I believed that my body was less detectable than those white figures everywhere around me. This was undoubtedly a self-sense that was enhanced by my pot smoking proclivities, the slightly paranoid flights of fancy of a stoner. But I came a decade later to learn that it was also in crucial part due to the fact that I was visually impaired and had long since needed glasses. One of my eyes is much weaker than the other; the right eye struggles to see and is dependent on the left for visual sense-making. I was not seeing the world clearly, and so I conceptually reversed the problem by imagining that it was the world that was incapable of seeing me. Perhaps it has always gone both ways.

Do I see the other woman clearly? Certainly not. But is my conjuring of her, however fantastical, a kind of truth? Am I myself seen, and if so, by whom? Whatever the case may be, I feel that I have become part of a womanish assemblage, collectively linked through our contact with

91

S we comprise an archive of gendered bodies, dispersed across time and geography but no less entwined.

The women S loved before me have known his body in various states of masculinity. It is a body that has morphed over time in ways that have shifted organically and been surgically and chemically transformed. And he has known each of us as becoming-bodies too. Can any of our bodies be said to be the same bodies now? There are multiple ways of answering this question. But none of them alter the distinct feeling that we are linked, we women, through a shared repository of his contact.

I HAVE BEEN HEDGING for months now on writing about S, feeling an embodied yet opaque obstacle in my path. She is the future-other-woman, both a body and a sign that I have been broken. She is me but comes after. Like me, she will pour through the archive in search of his past, and among other traces she will find me – the queer voice of a hybrid who was the last one to have lived the world with him. I worry over her, and already love her. I want to reach out to her from the present, which is also the past, to say: "The fact of you means the thing I love is broken." I want to articulate to her my devastation in advance. But also, and crucially, to welcome her lovingly into this genealogy of womanliness to which she will belong.

AMONG THE ODD THINGS about long-distance love in the virtual age is that it is all virtual, and then it is all physical, until it becomes all virtual again. We spent our second weekend together in a frenzy of uninhibited fucking, getting lost in enamored distraction every time we left the apartment. As I pulled away from his Brooklyn sublet in a Lyft, he renewed our text exchange by writing "come back!" instantly followed by another message which read: "You're in every room of this apartment."

An hour later, rolling down the east coast on Amtrak's Silver Star, I was feeling the absence of his body and reaching out for it. I finger-tapped into being a fragmented note, an acknowledgment that I could think of nothing other than him:

> I begin to gather the present archive, the now-making assembly through which I become enamored with one who is threshold: brother-sister, art maker, queer punk, architect of feel. You. So perfectly calculated in your willingness to dislodge, to make alternate life flourish. You are making something for and with me. Something I can't yet discern. A makeshift record of my bodily spill, your voice, a fridge filled with sub-par leftovers, an unexceptional piece of shell that is also my body, the tools you have used on other beautiful bodies and now mine. This is our archive. It clamors against my every hush.

Knowing that the content did not fit the form, I touched the arrow icon and sent the missive into space, a disembodied note that was also an embodied promise. It was all another way of saying something simple: "I want to burrow so deep in language with you that we exceed it."

The Ghost Archive

Early in Leslie Feinberg's queer classic *Stone Butch Blues,*
the protagonist Jess narrates the setting of her birth.
What she tells is her mother's story, a story echoed across
Jess's childhood, one that thus comes to constitute her
own sense of being. The story, in sum, is this: Trapped
alone inside her apartment during a fierce storm, Jess's
mother weeps loudly in labor. Hearing these sounds of
distress, the Dineh women who live across the hall inter-
vene to help birth the baby. When they offer the newborn
over to its mother, she responds with a chilling declarative: "Put the baby over there."[1]

Reading this passage aloud to my students, I was suddenly drawn headlong into my own history, as Jess observes
that the "story was retold many times as I was growing
up, as though the frost that bearded those words could
be melted by repeating them in a humorous, ironic way."[2]

My mother narrates a similarly chilling albeit recurring
scene from my own youth. It unfolds in the late 1970s, in
the context of a mixed-race and oftentimes violent fam-

1   Leslie Feinberg, *Stone Butch Blues* (2014), 8, http://www.lesliefein-
    berg.net/download/479/. First published in 1993 by Firebrand Books.
2   Ibid.

ily. "When you were young," my mother says, "you used to scream at the edge of your playpen and tear out your hair, offering it to me in clumps, fistful after fistful." My mother smiles when she relays this story, chuckles at what a difficult child I was, without ever folding into the narrative the conditions under which a child would become so brutally self-destructive... "As though the frost that bearded those words could be melted by repeating them in a humorous, ironic way."

I metabolized this story over time, offering it over one day to my therapist in a tone that unconsciously replicates my mother's humorous retelling. My therapist cannot conceal her distress, taken aback by the whimsy with which I can relay a story of my own early trauma. She responds with an assertion: "You did not yet have language through which to articulate your distress." My hair was a stand-in for my anguish, each strand a word I had not yet learned, but needed urgently to give over.

Like Jess, my memory of this early scene is fabricated through repetitive maternal narrations. The stories that comprise us have left us both wanting more, wishing we had access to a fuller narrative frame. I call this wishing-wanting desire "the ghost archive." Everything we need to know but cannot know as we keep circling and sniffing around the edges. Everything that keeps affecting us and affecting others through us. Everything that remains right there, but just out of reach.

ACCORDING TO PSYCHOANALYSIS, THE true origin of our obsessive behaviors exists in the unconscious. Freud calls those things that appear to disappear, those things that are invisible yet no less inscribed in us, *permanent memory-traces*. They are our unidentified ghosts making themselves queerly manifest. One of the primary frustrations of psychoanalysis, at least from the vantage point of the couch, is that we cannot ultimately access the root of our obsessions. The unconscious is the most evasive archive of all, yet is pulsing right there inside you.

REPLETE WITH MEMORY-TRACES, I am all feeling and response. Each time my therapist returns me to my childhood, she asks me to image my own daughter in my place. To imagine my own daughter trying to reach me by tearing out her hair in screaming fistfuls. Each time I undertake this exercise, I discover myself to be a deep and enduring fracture. Each time, I am undone.

I HAVE AN ACUTE memory of my mother as a child, desperately lonely on the shores of Belfast. She is gathering treasures from the sea. At age 4, she is all blustering whiteness with full rosy cheeks. She has been sent away to boarding school and is crushed by the absence of her parents. She brushes a long strand of hair from her face, looks out into a distance that appears eternal. She seems to know, even then, that she will cross an ocean, that she is destined to transport her solitude to another continent.

Somewhere in this memory there is an overseer, a body who is making sure that my mother is not swallowed up by the sea. But whoever she is, she is well beyond the frame.

THE ONE I ONCE pushed from my body turns five. To commemorate this life-shift, we embark on an off-season road trip to North Carolina's Outer Banks to undertake a shell hunting expedition. What we search for is whole and swirl; what we find is fractured yet stunning. I think of this child, who is herself a fragment of my body. And my own body, which is also fragment. Something born, something shattered, something that articulates its interest in a mythical whole.

The ocean's calculus, scattered bits, everything evidence of a once-was. These once creaturely homes have been smashed into smallness. I walk through intense gusts of cool wind, a desiring seeker. We have come with the aim of finding a whole, special thing. The longer I search, the more I realize the fantasy of it, the more I believe in the meaning of fragment. Of these infinite, fractured oceanic offerings, I cull a triangular piece of clam shell. Its exterior unspectacular, save for the fact that I discover on it a wet groove the precise color of my skin. On the inside, another color altogether – that of a well-earned bruise.

Nature is repeating itself, repeating me. What if we could choose our injuries? What shapes would we become?

This oceanic bruise is a queer gift I want to give to S – a way of speaking something beneath language. To offer it is pure risk of being spit out as a broken thing. So instead, I tuck it away as a fantasy offering. Folded into my clothing, it is the material remnant of a gorgeous whole I never was. Soon, I will instruct S with precision on how I want his body to open mine, on how to handle the bruised fragment.

INTO THE WIND AND waves, my child dances across the beach as she calls to me: *Amma! Amma! Amma!*

What I hear is bird: *Caw! Caw! Caw!* A simple reminder that she is animal, that her mother listens through queer tongues.

MY CHILD IS SPECIES-PROMISCUOUS; she refuses to stay human. She becomes other-animal, forms herself into strange hybrids. She has not yet learned to be a girl. "Yes," I think, "why would you want to stay breached in the jerk and stall of the thing you were told to be?"

"I WANT TO BE a boy," my child declares off-handedly.

"What does it mean to be a boy?" I wonder in reply.

"It means you have a penis." To procure one, she explains, you simply defecate, retrieve a piece of feces, and stitch it to your vagina. I am struck by the ease of this formulation, and deeply impressed by the vision. I feel strangely satisfied – as though my child has offered a gift of reassurance that she will find ways to craft herself into what she desires or needs to become.

And then, amidst this maternal satisfaction, I feel a sudden spill of parental pedagogy surging from my body as postscript: "Vaginal contact with fecal matter can lead to infection, love. This you must always remember."

OVER BRUNCH IN FORT Greene with an intimate friend who is a beautiful witch, I make a small but no less prescient discovery about myself. My friend has ordered a dish which arrives with three distinct chutneys. One of these chutneys she especially loves, and immediately upon tasting it begins to seek out our server to ask for more. Oddly, I try to stop her, suggesting that what she was given is the limit of what she will be allowed. Surprised by my response, and recognizing it as part of my core, she looks at me squarely and says: "Why would you not ask for more of what you love most?"

She recognizes something I have not yet known of myself – that very rarely am I able to express straightforwardly my desires. I come at them sideways, I skim their margins. I chew on her question well beyond our brunch, imagining a world in which I could easily articulate my desire.

But is it really so simple to stitch desire into language? To do so presupposes that you have an archive of desire ready on your tongue. My desires are often molecular, little creatures not yet prepared to leave my body.

I AM DRAWN TO the ear, to the orifice that listens and sta-
bilizes most acutely. The part of the body that modulates
social cacophonies, that sometimes selects what it allows
in and at other times cannot help but to metabolize the
noise that surrounds it. The unexpected place where the
body's equilibrium is produced.

In Harry Dodge and Silas Howard's queer buddy film *By
Hook or By Crook,* Shy and Valentine develop a form of be-
ing-together that modulates social noise, uniting against
a world that punishes their difference. In a crucial scene,
Valentine (Dodge) begins to psychically unravel. Shy
(Howard) searches for something that might calm his
friend – a piece of gum, a cup of coffee – until Valentine
asks simply: "Can you get my ears?" In this stunning moment, Shy answers his friend's strange request and begins to rub Valentine's acoustic orifices. What touch is
this? Poised behind his friend, Shy hovers carefully over
Valentine, engaging an act of reparation, of unabashed
love in radical embrace of freak friendship. I return often
to this cinematic memory of unexpected contact – a uto-
pian document in the scattered archive of transformative
touch.

I become ever more preoccupied with this notion of
transformative touch between friends. With contact that
cannot be reduced to the normative cultural paradigms
– sexual and parental – of intimate touch. What kinds of
touch live beyond these paradigms, making up dissenting communities? The touch I desire most intensely is
the touch of the friend that folds me into collective alterity, that feels and shapes me as an anti-normative social
body. A misfit thing held and felt by other misfit things.

MY FIRST SUMMER IN the United States was spent studying Hindi in California. Wandering home at dusk on my
second night in South Berkeley, I was suddenly surround-
ed by four boys wielding a machete. I had on my body a
newly attained set of apartment keys, my ID, a pocket-
sized copy of *The Communist Manifesto*, a bag of organic
produce from the Berkeley Bowl, and a DVD of *Sense and
Sensibility*.

This last item was my downfall. I had lingered too long
in the aisles of Reel Video, embarrassed to be checking
out a Victorian film. By the time I left the video store the
sun was waning. I saw the boys from a distance, so clearly
conspiring toward something, looking poly-directionally
for some form of access-making. I thought of the native
kids I had spent years entertaining at a recreation center
in Winnipeg, where I worked to pay my way through college. To those kids, I was a gatekeeper that could offer
respite from the street; to these other searching boys, I
was another kind of opportunity altogether.

The boys let me pass, then split up – two staying behind,
two running ahead to circle back and surround the object I had become. The strategy was clever and quick. The
oldest boy stood behind me in a strange embrace. The
front of his body was wedged against my back, almost intimately, as his arms wrapped around my waist to edge
a machete against my stomach. "Don't move girl, don't
move," he whispered in my ear. Almost a hum, but there
was a shake to it. The others searched my body hard and
fast for removable things. I had never seen a machete
before: I learned this object through the encounter. I
learned it with a hard precision.

I knew there was no way out, so instead of plotting an
escape I wondered over the event, the extent of the damage. I thought of rape, because one must in such situ-

ations. But it was too public a space, there wouldn't be time for it. I felt the blade press harder into my stomach, as though it was its own actor yearning to get inside my body. Then just as suddenly as it had all started, the boys disbanded, and the machete too. The second the blade and bodies had extricated themselves, words started tumbling out of my body. What surfaced was the tongue-lashing of an older sister, a would-be mother. I wanted them to know we were still linked. And in some delusion of agency, I commanded them in vain to drop my ID, to leave my apartment keys.

I watched them all fade around a corner and realized that the smallest of the boys, the little runt, was doubling back boldly to snatch my groceries. He had something to prove, to show his buddies that he was a player. I studied his body as a thing in motion as it returned to me, and in exasperation I asked: "Really?! You're going to jump a girl *and* steal her groceries?!" The runt's diminutive body was running, running, running, but just before he rounded a corner to vanish forever, he turned back to me and hollered so sweetly and sincerely: "I'm sorry, ma'am!"

In my memory of this scene, there are only objects and words, words as objects. The weapon and the apology – have they ever been discrete?

Moments later, I approached the first house I saw with lights on and knocked at the door. An older white couple peered through the window but would not open the door. I told them that I had been jumped and having spoken the words my body promptly started to shake and sob. They left me on their doorstep alone, locking themselves in while they called the cops from the safety of their bourgeois abode.

An older white cop arrived and pronounced my assailants "Oakland boys." Though I was new to the United States and knew nothing about Oakland, I understood clearly that what he meant was that they were poor and black. I started to rehearse what I knew about the racial politics of the American criminal justice system, something I had studied as an undergraduate in an introductory sociology course in Winnipeg. He responded with intolerance toward the kind of victim I was – an impossible alien – and immediately called in a younger black cop, Officer W. Officer W spent the next several hours with me, combing the streets for my stolen things while we waited for a locksmith to let me back inside my sublet. "They had a choice, and they made a bad one," he insisted. "I could have chosen that path too, but I chose instead to fight against it." I knew that this formulation was twisted, that Officer W understood the world as a binary structure of good guys and bad guys, and that all it took for him was personal conviction to end up in the right place, otherwise known as law enforcement.

The following day, still feeling terrified and alone, I called a graduate school friend for support. Hearing the story, he brazenly asserted (in that particular white-masculine-American way) that the boys had chosen me as their prey because I "looked like an immigrant, an easy target." I felt enraged and betrayed, perhaps as much by my friend as by the schizophrenic logics through which America frames itself.

IN SECOND GRADE MUSIC class, a curly-haired white boy looks at me squarely and says: "You would have been pretty if you were white." My fist becomes a mind that curls into a ball and hurtles itself toward his face. When asked by the principle the motive for my crime, I can feel my fist thinking, and lose every single word I have learned.

Later in my youth, meandering down Broadway, a thin man walks toward me, gathers phlegm in his mouth, and hocks it with immaculate precision onto my small brown face. His saliva edges down my cheek. It seems to be feeling me out, trying to find its way in. Again, my language vanishes.

Words and spit mingling with flesh and feeling, leaving such palpable traces. A little girl's body becoming the imprint of history, the sensation of something penetrative being reproduced.

AT SOME IMPRECISE MOMENT of my childhood, my mother inherited a portrait painted by a German Jewish ancestor, Leopold Guterbock. The painting was hung in our dining room, where it still hangs today in a heavy gilded frame so ornate it seems to compete for attention with the painting it encases. The portrait is of a girl, perhaps five years old, almost porcelain save for her rosy cheeks. Her white dress falls sensually from an unusually round, bare shoulder. The background is almost black, but my mother was at pains to show us that tucked in the girl's arms, almost as dark as the background itself, is a very small monkey. A little pet captured from the colonies, a far less agential version of Kafka's Red Peter.

I cannot begin to calculate the hours of my youth spent in the presence of this image, an image I found myself uneasily tethered to. So utterly alien, the portrait seemed to be speaking to me – a ghostly, opaque summoning. But whose ghost was calling me? Was it the girl, whom I no doubt longed to be? Or was it the nearly imperceptible monkey in her arms, snatched from a place of deep belonging? Each choice is a decision, and the tether is ultimately undecidable.

Upon returning home last summer, I stood before the portrait with my mother. She was astonished to find that I had, after all of these years, thought the portrait to be Ferdinand's work. She now insisted that though it bore his imprint, it was in fact painted by his wife and my namesake, Julie Rebecca Guterbock. She then pointed to a fierce gash in the wall that emanated from behind the portrait and ran down to the floor. It was the lingering evidence of how the girl and her monkey had recently tried to break free, leaving an undeniable trace of their flight before my mother had them reaffixed to the wall.

CONDUCTING HER RESEARCH ON Arthur Munby's photographs of working-class women in the archive at Trinity
College, the art historian Carol Mavor describes being es-
corted by two men into a room, where she is given a pair
of clean white gloves. A silk cloth is laid before her on a
table, and the Munby box is then revealed to her. Before
she opens it, she must slip her hands into the gloves to
become a traceless thing. There is a rich eroticism at work
in this performative unfolding.

Once inside the box, Mavor is consumed by images of
Hannah Cullwick, a 19th-century English servant who
masqueraded ubiquitously – as Magdalene, as a Black
slave, as a chimney-sweep, as a gentleman, as a proper
lady. Hannah slips between purity and filth, working history against itself through her body. The historian fingers
the archive, following the rules of the library. Yet somehow and undeniably she is engaged in an act of trespass.
But of what threshold?

The more I return to this scene, the more I attend to the
erotic relay at work. The photographer's erotic desire for
his subject, which becomes the historian's erotic desire
for her archived object, until finally the historian's relation to the images becomes the object of my own desiring
mind. All this lust becoming the archive itself.

A TEACHER OF MY youth used to utter compulsively the refrain "curiosity killed the cat." In my elementary school yearbook, he inscribed a message: "You ask questions incessantly without waiting to hear the answers." An inscription of the teacher's sheer frustration with a student teaching herself, at the audacity of putting language in the air without the need to foreclose it.

"To emancipate someone else," writes Jacques Rancière, "one must be emancipated oneself. One must know oneself to be a voyageur of the mind, similar to all other voyageurs: an intellectual subject participating in the power common to all intellectual beings."[3] Only this knowing, he argues, can make for a liberationist pedagogy. The less you have mastered knowledge, the better apt you are to let others learn themselves.

3   Jacques Rancière, *The Ignorant Schoolmaster*, trans. Kristin Ross (Stanford: Stanford University Press, 1991), 33.

I WAKE THIS MORNING and want to learn the history of burning books. I want to study every public decision to transform ideas into ash, to feel the trace of those remains. The burnt book is a body that has been made, and then made to hurt. In her poem "The Burning of Paper Instead of Children," Adrienne Rich writes: "The burning of the book arouses no sensation in me. I know it hurts to burn."[4] I, too, know it hurts to burn, to transform into ash, yet in response I am all sensation.

The burnt book is a social text, a public performance of disavowal. This burning is a desire to forget what is already lodged within the collective, but which cannot be comfortably acknowledged therein. The burnt book is a fear of monsters, an urgent public need to destroy them: political manifestos, novels, children's stories, pornography – all made cinder and smoke.

I once scoffed at this fear, that contact with difference would slip into contagion. But now I anticipate the contagion, opening my body to the surround. This opening is both welcome and protest. Not merely an acceptance of the outside, but a willful desire to let it in, to recognize that it has always already been here.

I wake and want to study the burnt book from its inception to its end: first as idea, then labor, then tree, then press, then smoke, then ash, then scatter. I want to sense what Erin Manning calls the "anarchive," that strange and stunning "something that catches us in our own becoming."[5] This is the future archive. The archive of alterity. And like yours and mine, it is a body that has

---

4 Adrienne Rich, "The Burning of Paper Instead of Children," in *The Fact of a Doorframe* (New York: W.W. Norton & Co., 1984), 116–19.

5 Erin Manning, *For a Pragmatics of the Useless* (Durham: Duke University Press, forthcoming 2019).

gone up in flame. A body that is in excess, that is another world and also this one.